ELEMENTS

OF

CRISIS

INTERVENTION

CRISES & HOW TO RESPOND TO THEM

James L. Greenstone
Diplomate, American Board of Examiners in Crisis Intervention

Sharon C. Leviton
Diplomate, American Board of Examiners in Crisis Intervention

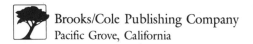 Brooks/Cole Publishing Company
Pacific Grove, California

I**T**P ™
The trademark ITP is used under license.

We dedicate this book to our colleagues Edward S. Rosenbluh,
Ph.D., and W. Rodney Fowler, Ed.D., pioneers in the field
of Crisis Management. Over the years we have taught alongside
them, and we continue to learn from them. Thanks, guys!

 A CLAIREMONT BOOK

Brooks/Cole Publishing Company
A Division of Wadsworth, Inc.

© 1993 by Wadsworth, Inc., Belmont, California 94002.

Printed in the United States of America
10 9 8 7 6

Library of Congress Cataloging-in-Publication Data

Greenstone, James L.
  The elements of crisis intervention / James L. Greenstone, Sharon
C. Leviton.
    p.   cm.
  Includes bibliographical references.
  ISBN 0-534-19908-9
  1. Crisis intervention (Psychiatry)   I. Leviton, Sharon.
II. Title.
RC480.6.G719 1993
362.2'04251—dc20   92-36153
                                                        CIP

Sponsoring Editor: *Claire Verduin*
Editorial Associate: *Gay C. Bond*
Production Editor: *Penelope Sky*
Manuscript Editor: *Laurie Vaughn*
Interior and Cover Design: *Leesa Berman*
Art Coordinator: *Susan Haberkorn*
Interior Illustration: *Susan Haberkorn*
Typesetting: *Bookends Typesetting*
Printing and Binding: *Malloy Lithographing, Inc.*

ABOUT THE AUTHORS

JAMES L. GREENSTONE

Dr. James L. Greenstone is the Fort Worth, Texas, Police Department Psychologist. Since 1966 he has been a marriage and family psychotherapist and a family dispute mediator in private practice in Dallas, Texas. Dr. Greenstone is National Vice President of the American Academy of Crisis Interveners and the chairman of the American Board of Examiners in Crisis Intervention. He is president of the Southwestern Academy of Crisis Interveners and Editor-in-Chief of *The Journal of Crisis Intervention*. He is also a fellow of the Southeastern Academy of Crisis Interveners and in 1981 received their Distinguished Service Award.

Dr. Greenstone has been a deputy sheriff with the Dallas County Sheriff's Department Reserve and an instructor at the Sheriff's Training Academy; he has worked with the Tactical Team and the Criminal Investigation Division in hostage negotiations. He has also served as a consultant to the Detentions Bureau in Crisis Management, counseling supervision, and the inmate drug abuse program.

In 1982, Dr. Greenstone received the Distinguished Service Award for Life Saving from the Reserve Law Officer's Association of America. A police lieutenant from 1986 to 1992 with the Lancaster, Texas, police department, he was Reserve Training Officer and implemented the department's Hostage Negotiations Team. He is fully certified as a peace officer in the State of Texas and holds police instructor certificates from Texas, Alaska, and Florida.

Dr. Greenstone has been the senior editor of the *Crisis Intervener's Newsletter* and Editor-in-Chief of the journal *Emotional First Aid*. He is the author or coauthor of the *Crisis*

Intervener's Handbook; Hotline: A Crisis Intervention Directory; Crisis Intervention: Handbook for Interveners; Winning Through Accommodation: The Mediator's Handbook; and *The Crisis Intervention Compendium.* Audiocassette series include *Crisis Management and Intervener Survival; Stress Reduction: Personal Energy Management;* and *Training the Trainer.* Dr. Greenstone has also contributed chapters to *Innovative Psychotherapies* (edited by Raymond Corsini) and *The Wiley Encyclopedia of Psychology.*

SHARON C. LEVITON

Dr. Sharon C. Leviton holds degrees in Education and Crisis Intervention, and is an individual and family psychotherapist, family dispute mediator, and crisis specialist in private practice in Dallas, Texas. She is vice chairman of the American Board of Examiners in Crisis Intervention, executive director of the Southwestern Academy of Crisis Interveners, and a fellow of both the American Academy of Crisis Interveners and the Southeastern Academy of Crisis Interveners.

Dr. Leviton has edited the *Crisis Intervener's Newsletter* and the journal *Emotional First Aid.* She is the coauthor of *The Crisis Intervener's Handbook; Hotline: A Crisis Intervention Directory; Crisis Intervention: Handbook for Interveners;* and *Winning Through Accommodation: The Mediator's Handbook.* Audiocassette series include *Crisis Management and Intervener Survival; Stress Reduction: Personal Energy Management;* and *Training the Trainer.* She has contributed chapters to *Innovative Psychotherapies* (edited by Raymond Corsini), *The Wiley Encyclopedia of Psychology,* and *The Crisis Intervention Compendium* (edited by W. Rodney Fowler). She has written articles, papers, and editorials about psychotherapy, Crisis Intervention, stress management, and family and marital dispute mediation.

PREFACE

The Elements of Crisis Intervention is intended for the following groups of people.

Crisis workers
Hot-line workers
Parents
Teachers
Counselors and psychotherapists
Support group members and leaders
Outreach groups
Police officers
Probation and parole officers
Peer counselors
Teenage support groups
Attorneys
Emergency medical service personnel
Fire fighters
Bartenders

We have reduced the practice of Crisis Intervention to its basic elements so they can be applied as broadly as possible, and we present them in a format that is useful both for the experienced professional and for the novice. We know of no other text that approaches the subject so directly. We have spent much time in our careers eliminating confusion about procedures and about the relationship between Crisis Intervention and other behavioral sciences. This book reinforces the theoretical framework that postulates Crisis Intervention as a viable discipline in itself.

Because this is a practical guide, most theory has been purposely omitted. We suggest that *Elements of Crisis Intervention* be used as a supplement in classes in psychology, counseling, psychotherapy, crisis intervention, crisis counseling, health services, emergency medicine, police science, negotiations, and in other related practical and applied courses at all levels. It is also appropriate for training courses in Crisis Intervention and Crisis Counseling. The experienced intervener can use the book independently, in the classroom, in the office, and in the field.

HOW TO USE THIS BOOK

This book is designed to aid in practical, day-to-day, on-the-scene Crisis Intervention. In addition to listing the areas covered in the chapters, the table of contents is a step-by-step guide to the intervention process, and should be used by interveners to guide an intervention in an orderly fashion. For the experienced crisis intervener, the table of contents is a helpful reminder of the steps to be taken during an intervention. Novices may need to read the entire book carefully before they can use the table of contents effectively, and they should understand that the full value of this book depends on their gaining theoretical depth and practical training.

Interveners can also look up material according to the activity they want to perform, and by the intervener's role (for example, police officer or therapist). These listings are printed on the inside of the front and back cover of the book.

THE ELEMENTS OF
CRISIS INTERVENTION

A crisis occurs when unusual stress temporarily renders an individual unable to direct life effectively. As the stress mounts and the usual coping mechanisms provide neither relief nor remedy, the person often experiences extreme feelings of fear, anger, grief, hostility, helplessness, hopelessness, and alienation from self, family, and society. Stress can be a reaction to a single event or to several events occurring simultaneously or serially.

Ordinary upsets can be handled with day-to-day skills. Crises happen suddenly and unexpectedly and seem arbitrary. Inexplicable events raise stress to a critical level. Crisis Intervention is a timely and skillful intrusion into a personal crisis in order to defuse a potentially disastrous situation before physical or emotional destruction occurs. The intervener attempts to return the sufferer to a level of pre-crisis functioning at a time when his or her life lacks structure. Rosenbluh (1975) calls this "emotional first aid." Just as people bleed physically, they can also bleed—and bleed to death—emotionally. Crisis Intervention is not therapy. It is the skilled attempt to stop the emotional bleeding in a way that will allow the individual to continue life effectively. The intervener makes quick, accurate, critical decisions about the victim and mobilizes needed resources. Successful Crisis Intervention achieves problem management, not problem resolution. The intervener who has helped the victim of a crisis regain pre-crisis stability has met the goals of Crisis Intervention. Although an individual may require support after a crisis that can include psychotherapy or counseling, effective Crisis Intervention can significantly reduce the need for intensive treatment.

To a great extent, we apply the theory that "A crisis is a crisis is a crisis" (Leviton, 1982, p. 10). Although one can certainly argue that a particular incident requires a specific response, that incident-specific response is always grounded in the basic Crisis Intervention theory and procedures that are the subject of this book. As Rosenbluh puts it, "If we are to be helpful, we must remain effective" (1975), and the keys to effectiveness are clear understanding of the elements of Crisis Intervention and the ability to apply them practically. A return to the basics is nearly always beneficial, and is continually instructive, to all who labor in the vineyard of conflict management.

James L. Greenstone
Sharon C. Leviton

CONTENTS

Chapter Five
INTERVENER SURVIVAL   39

1. Recognize the signs and symptoms of stress and burnout.
2. Take care of yourself.
    a. Eat nutritiously.
    b. Get enough rest.
    c. Exercise regularly.
    d. Set realistic goals for yourself..
    e. Plan for fun and relaxation.
    f. Be responsible for self-direction.
    g. Be concerned about personal safety.
3. Become aware of your own personal issues.

Chapter Six
CHILDREN'S REACTION TO CRISIS   45

1. Teachers: Take care of yourselves and each other.
2. Learn the "typical" reactions of normal children in each age group.
3. Refer the family for professional help as needed.
4. Create age- and grade-appropriate activities for children in crisis.
    a. Preschool
    b. Elementary School
    c. Junior and Senior High School
        (1) Journalism
        (2) Science
        (3) English Composition
        (4) Literature
        (5) Psychology

Chapter Seven

HOT-LINE WORKERS 61

1. Learn the Do's to effective hot-line interactions.
2. Avoid the Don'ts that can lead to ineffective hot-line interactions.
3. Learn to handle the difficult caller.

Chapter Eight

FAMILY CRISIS 67

1. Follow the thirty steps for handling family crisis.
2. Learn how parents can help their children cope with crisis-related feelings.
3. In preparing for holidays, follow the twenty steps for avoiding holiday crisis.

Chapter Nine

GRIEF 75

1. Look for the grief component in the crisis.
2. Recognize what grief victims may experience.

3. Teach the sufferer to use self-intervention.
4. Help the sufferer cope with separation or loss.
5. Recognize the recurring reactions of sufferers of tragic events.

1. Know the laws that may govern what you do.
2. Treat victims as human beings rather than as cases.
3. Intervene within the limits of your background, training, and experience.
4. If you begin an intervention, stay with it unless you are relieved by someone with greater skill.
5. If possible, obtain consent before intervening.
6. Maintain confidentiality of all information you obtain.
7. Document all your actions in an intervention.
8. Maintain your professional competency.
9. Respect the victim's right to privacy.
10. Think before you act.

CHAPTER ONE

APPROACH TO CRISIS INTERVENTION

WHAT IS A CRISIS?

Crisis results from stress and tension in a person's life. Stress is the key element in crisis development. As stress mounts to unusual proportions and the individual's coping skills become increasingly ineffective, the potential for crisis occurs. The *crisis cube* is a three-dimensional representation of crisis development (see Figure 1.1). The crisis cube illustrates how, before a crisis, the normal level of functioning can be interrupted by the occurrence of unusual stress due to single, multiple, or serial factors. When this happens, one attempts to solve problems and handle tension in usual ways. As this fails, a downward spiral of ineffective behavior, referred to as *maladaptive behavior*, occurs. Crisis Intervention is the act of interrupting the downward spiral as skillfully and as quickly as possible and, in so doing, of returning the victim to a pre-crisis level of coping. As the time line on the crisis cube indicates, every moment is crucial to the intervener. The longer the line of maladaptive behavior goes unchallenged and uninterrupted,

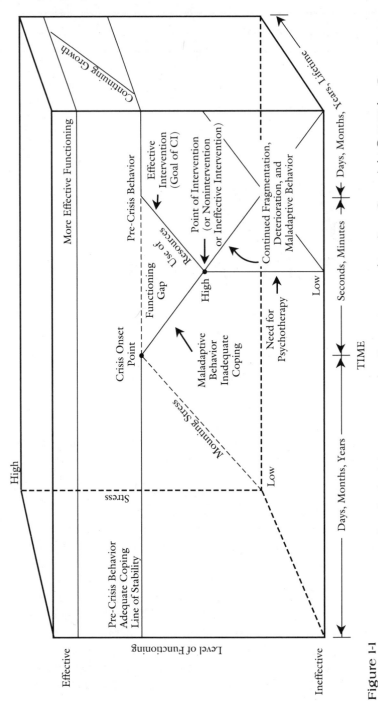

Figure 1-1
The Crisis Cube. From Handbook of Crisis Interveners by Greenstone and Leviton. Copyright © 1982 by Greenstone. Reprinted with permission of Kendall/Hunt Publishing Co.

2

the greater the possibility of increased personality disintegration and increased need for psychological treatment or therapy after the crisis is over. The intervener's skill and the timeliness of the intervention can determine the possibility of the victim's later functioning and growth.

Crisis Intervention (or Crisis Management) and counseling (or psychotherapy) must be separated in terms of function and application. Crisis Intervention/Management is an attempt to deal quickly with an immediate problem. Often it requires providing for victims that which the victims cannot provide for themselves. This can include a physical or emotional crutch to lean on, and even direction by the intervener at a time in the victim's life when self-direction may be impossible. Crisis Intervention is to emergency-room medicine what a medical practice is to a psychotherapy practice. Psychotherapy and Crisis Intervention must never be confused. To do so could deny victims what they need at a very critical time in their lives. To be sure, every therapist will benefit from developing Crisis Intervention skills, but to assume that Crisis Intervention and counseling are the same is courting disaster (see Corsini, 1981).

Psychotherapy, crisis counseling, short-term psychotherapy, or other forms of therapeutic intervention may be appropriate after Crisis Intervention. Interveners should make no assumptions about helping the victim find solutions to the problems that precipitated the crisis. Management, not resolution, is the intervener's goal, and at best it is a very short-term one. If the victim needs care after intervention, referral for appropriate short- or long-term therapeutic involvement is the additional responsibility of the intervener. Rosenbluh (1981) refers to Crisis Intervention as "emotional first aid." Crisis Intervention is the emotional equivalent of physical first aid and must be applied in the same skillful and timely fashion to allow victims to maximize their involvement in psychotherapy or counseling if required.

The following are indicators of a person who may be prone to crisis. A list of precipitating factors is also presented. Finally, signs and symptoms of a person in crisis are presented as a guide to recognition of and need for intervention. These events must be understood from the sufferers' perspectives of what a crisis is for them.

INDICATORS THAT CAN CHARACTERIZE A CRISIS-PRONE PERSON

1. Alienation from lasting and meaningful personal relationships
2. Inability to use life support systems such as family, friends, and social groups
3. Difficulty in learning from experience; the individual continues to make the same mistakes
4. A history of previously experienced crises that have not been effectively resolved
5. A history of mental disorder or severe emotional imbalance
6. Feelings of low self-esteem
7. Provocative, impulsive behavior resulting from unresolved inner conflict
8. A history of poor marital relationships
9. Excessive use of drugs, including alcohol abuse
10. Marginal income
11. Lack of regular, fulfilling work
12. Unusual or frequent physical injuries
13. Frequent changes in residence
14. Frequent encounters with the law

EVENTS THAT CAN PRECIPITATE A CRISIS

1. An accident in the home
2. An automobile accident, with or without injury
3. Being arrested; appearing in court
4. Changes in job situation and income involving either promotion or demotion
5. Change in school status
6. Death of a significant person in one's life
7. Divorce or separation

8. A delinquency episode either in childhood or adulthood (In childhood: skipping school or running away from home; in adulthood: failure to pay debts)
9. Entry into school
10. Abortion or out-of-wedlock pregnancy
11. Physical illness
12. Acute episodes of mental disorder
13. Retirement
14. Natural disasters
15. Sexual difficulties
16. Major change in living conditions
17. Gaining a new family member (for example, through birth, adoption, or parents or adult children moving in)
18. Dealing with a blended family
19. Foreclosure on a mortgage or loan
20. Actual or impending loss of something significant in one's life

Although a particular stressful situation may not induce crisis, a combination of several such stressful events may push the individual to the crisis point.

RECOGNIZING A PERSON IN CRISIS
1. Recognition depends on:
   a. Intervener's awareness of what the victim is communicating verbally and nonverbally
   b. Intervener's sensing capabilities
2. Different people may indicate crisis in different ways:
   a. Crying out, exploding, verbalizing
   b. Withdrawal, depression, or both
3. If possible, the intervener should obtain information from family and friends about the victim's pre-crisis behavior and note disruptions in previous behavior, as well as modes of ineffective functioning.
4. Profile of a person in crisis:
   a. *Bewilderment:* "I never felt this way before."
   b. *Danger:* "I am so nervous and scared."

    c. *Confusion:* "I can't think clearly."
    d. *Impasse:* "I feel stuck; nothing I do helps."
    e. *Desperation:* "I've got to do something."
    f. *Apathy:* "Nothing can help me."
    g. *Helplessness:* "I can't take care of myself."
    h. *Urgency:* "I need help now!!!!!!!!"
    i. *Discomfort:* "I feel miserable, restless, and unsettled."

At this point, the victim is not totally in control of life and feels the panic resulting from this realization. Victims may flail about emotionally, verbally, or even physically as they experience this lack of control.

COMMON SIGNS AND SYMPTOMS OF PSYCHOLOGICAL REACTIONS TO CRISIS

Emotional

anticipatory anxiety
generalized anxiety
shock
denial
insecurity
fatigue
uncertainty
fear
helplessness
depression
panic
despair
survivor guilt
feeling out of control
grief
outrage
numbness
frustration
inadequacy
feeling overwhelmed
anger
irritability

Cognitive
confusion
poor attention span
poor concentration
flashbacks
loss of trust
difficulties in decision making
nightmares
Behavioral
withdrawal
sleep disturbances
angry outbursts
change in activity
change in appetite
increased fatigue
excessive use of sick leave
alcohol or drug abuse
irritability
difficulty functioning at normal ability level
antisocial acts
frequent visits to physician for nonspecific complaints
anger at God
loss of desire to attend religious services
regression
crying
change in communications
preoccupation with the crisis to the exclusion of other
    areas of life
diminished job performance
unresponsiveness
hysterical reactions

CHAPTER TWO

PROCEDURE FOR EFFECTIVE CRISIS INTERVENTION

Crisis Intervention consists of six major components (see Figure 2.1):

    I. **Immediacy**
   II. **Control**
  III. **Assessment**
  IV. **Disposition**
   V. **Referral**
  VI. **Followup**

The following outlines detail the procedure for effective Crisis Intervention.

I. Act immediately to stop the emotional bleeding.

Intervention begins at the moment the intervener encounters the person in crisis. The intervener must immediately attempt to

- Relieve anxiety
- Prevent further disorientation

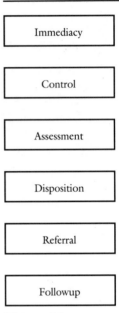

Figure 2.1
Crisis Intervention procedure

- Ensure that sufferers do not harm themselves or cause harm to others.

II. Take control.
  a. Be clear about what and whom you are attempting to control.

The purpose of assuming control is not to conquer or overwhelm the victim. Rather, it is to help reorder the chaos that exists in the sufferer's world at the moment of crisis. The intervener provides the needed structure until the victim is able to regain control.

  b. Enter the crisis scene cautiously.

Approach any crisis situation slowly and carefully. Caution at this point can prevent unnecessary grief. Take a moment to mentally compute what you

- hear
- see
- smell
- feel
- sense
- touch

    c. Appear stable, supportive, and able to establish structure.

Use your personal presence. Your strength, control, and calm in the crisis situation may exert the control the victim needs.

    d. Be clear in your introductory statements. The opening questions, directions, and other information you give the victim will often assist in gaining and in maintaining control.

Intervener: Hello, I'm Sharon Leviton from the Crisis Center. Are you Mrs. Jones?

Mrs. Jones: Yes. I don't know what you or anybody else can do. I just know . . . I can't stand it anymore.

Intervener: I'd like to listen to what's bothering you. May I come in?

    e. Do not promise things that might not happen. For example, don't say, "I can fix it. Everything will be all right." It might not be!

    f. Direct and arrange the pattern of standing and sitting to gain the victim's attention.

    g. Guide the sufferer with your eyes and voice rather than through physical force.

    h. Use physical force only as a last resort, and only if you are trained and authorized to use it.

    i. Remove the victim from the crisis situation if possible. Otherwise, remove the crisis from the victim.

    j. Be creative in taking control.

    k. Break eye contact between disputants.

    l. Separate the victims if necessary.

Specific ways of gaining control in a crisis situation vary, depending on the skills and abilities of the intervener. The task allows wide latitude for creativity. Possible ways of taking control include the following:

- Creating a loud noise to gain attention.
- Speaking in a quieter tone than the victim.
- Breaking eye contact between two disputants to reduce tension.
- Making an odd request: "May I see that book over there?"

Victims will respond to structure and to those who represent it if they sense it is genuine and not just a technique.

III. Assess the situation.

- What is troubling the victim now?
- Why did the person go into crisis at this particular time?
- Which problem among the ones that may be present is of immediate concern?
- Which problem must be dealt with before other problems can be handled?
- Which problem among the ones presented can be immediately managed?
- What variables will hinder the problem-management process?
- How can the intervener implement the most effective help in the least time?

To accomplish an effective assessment, do the following:

a. Evaluate on the spot. Don't wait.
b. Make the evaluation quick, accurate, and comprehensive enough to give a total picture.
c. Do not take a lengthy life history. Focus your assessment on the present crisis and the events that occurred within the last forty-eight hours. What were the precipitating events?

Intervener: Tell me what happened in the last few days.
Mary: I lost my job today.

Intervener: Your job was important to you.

Mary: Yes. I have to have it because my husband walked out on me yesterday.

Intervener: You seem very frightened.

Mary: I'm scared to death. My husband left me. I've got three little babies. My mom is dying of cancer, and I don't have a job. We're three months behind in the rent. I've got nowhere to turn. There's no way I'm going to make it. I've got nowhere to go, so I may as well end it. My kids would be better off. . . .

     d. Ask short, direct questions.

Intervener: How are you feeling, John?

John: I feel lost and strange.

Intervener: What do you mean by "strange"?

John: I can't explain it.

Intervener: Can you put another feeling with strange?

John: Hopeless. I can't find any way to cope with Judy's death.

     e. Ask questions one at a time.

     f. Allow the victim enough time to answer your questions.

Intervener: Did you ever feel this way before?

(Pause)

John: I can't think too clearly. That's what is so scary to me.

Intervener: Take your time, John. We're in no rush.

     g. Do not increase victims' confusion by bombarding them with many questions at once.

     h. Learn to accept discomfort with silence. Recognize the usefulness of silence in the intervention process.

     i. Interrupt the victim judiciously. You can use periodic interruptions to clarify, to check the accuracy and your understanding of the victim's statements, and simply to remind the victim of your interest in the problem. Interrupt no more often than absolutely necessary.

     j. Clarify the crisis.

Intervener: Your fear of your dad finding out about your pregnancy seems to be causing your feelings of terror.

Ann: That's most of it. I disappointed and embarrassed him. He'll abandon me. He'll slap my mom around and blame her. I ruined it for everybody! I've got to run away.

k. Allow the crisis to be the victim's crisis.

Avoid judgments, preachments, and putdowns. Don't belittle the victim or the crisis; crisis is always in the eye of the beholder. The way the victim currently perceives the world is the victim's reality. For example, don't say, "You're silly to be so worried. He wasn't worth it anyway. I know you'll find someone else next week."

l. Assess both the actual and the symbolic meaning of the crisis event. Remember that perception triggers crisis much more often than do facts.

m. Use the sufferer's body language and nonverbal behavior as a source of information. If you observe that the words and behavior do not match, question the discrepancy.

n. Listen for what is *not* being said. Attend to what the victim says and does. Be aware of what the victim has not done and what would normally be expected under current circumstances.

o. Recognize that your personal attributes contribute to your overall effectiveness.

- Remain reassuring and calm.
- Remain empathic and attentive.
- Remain supportive.
- Be willing to reach out to the sufferer, both physically and emotionally, as needed.
- Maintain a caring attitude that conveys a willingness to listen.

p. Allow the victim to speak freely and to ventilate feelings.

q. Help the victim to see the crisis as temporary rather than chronic.

 r. In a multiple-victim situation (such as a family dispute), allow each person to speak without interruption by the other people involved. Establish ground rules immediately, and insist they be followed.

Intervener: Mr. Jones, will you agree to listen while your wife talks to us?

Mr. Jones: But she never shuts up.

Intervener: I will ensure that each of you has enough time to say what you need to. I'm very interested in hearing both of you.

Mr. Jones: OK, I'll agree to that. But she better be careful. You have to watch her.

Intervener: Mrs. Jones, will you agree to listen while Mr. Jones talks?

Mrs. Jones: Oh, yes. You can count on me.

 s. Return control to the victim as soon as possible.

IV. Decide how to handle the situation after you have assessed it.

Heightened stress closes down options and generally produces "tunnel vision" in the victim. When effective intervention occurs, the victim becomes more receptive to

- exploring options
- thinking creatively
- solving problems

 a. Help the victim identify and mobilize personal resources.

Intervener: Mrs. Smith, what is one way that you might manage that trapped feeling when John is out of town?

Mrs. Smith: I can call the lady next door and trade baby-sitting with her.

Intervener: Would you feel comfortable with that?

Mrs. Smith: She's very caring and responsible, and it could be good for the kids and for me. I wouldn't get so angry and upset with the kids. I can't believe what I almost did.

Intervener: Do you have any other ideas?

Mrs. Smith: John and I need some professional help about a few things. Could you help me find a family counselor? I'm ready to get on with this.

Intervener: Yes, I can.

   b. Mobilize social resources.
   c. Hold out hope that solutions are possible.
   d. Develop options.
   e. Help the parties to the crisis make an agreement.

Almost any agreement answers the following questions:

Who?
What?
Where?
When?
Why?
What if?
How much?

Mr. Jones: I'll baby-sit on Tuesday evenings so Mary can take care of her dad.

Intervener: What time on Tuesday?

Mr. Jones: I can get home by 5:00 P.M. Remember, I can't keep this up after January.

Intervener: So, after January, Mary will have to make other plans about the visitation.

Mrs. Jones: I understand. The pressure should be over by then.

Intervener: What if you can't baby-sit on Tuesday at that time?

Mr. Jones: I'll be responsible for making other arrangements.

V. Refer as needed. Follow up if possible or as agreed.
   a. Investigate possible referral sources by checking local telephone directories and manuals that list specialized services.
   b. Check with professionals such as doctors, lawyers, and clergy in the community. Determine if they

take referrals from crisis situations; not all do. Ask if they would be on call to assist if needed.

c. Contact local hospital emergency care units and get to know the staff. Find out about requirements for admission and treatment.

d. Visit agencies in the community that provide assistance to crisis victims. Find out if they are willing and equipped to accept referrals and if they will
   (1) give a crisis-victim referral high priority in scheduling,
   (2) understand the need for proper crisis referrals, and
   (3) give feedback when an intervener tries to follow up on someone who has been referred.

e. Determine the hours of operation of each potential referral agency. Are they staffed by people or answering machines?

f. Make a list of acceptable referral sources.

g. Be sure the phone numbers, addresses, and names of contact persons are current.

h. Determine what state and national referral agencies or hot lines crisis victims can access.

i. Update your referral list regularly. Add reliable agencies once you have checked them. Eliminate unreliable agencies as your experience with each dictates. Delete agencies that no longer provide the needed crisis services.

j. Determine the required fees for services and acceptable methods of payment.

k. Determine which agencies will accept referrals of crisis victims with limited financial resources.

l. Know the availability of transportation to and from the referral source. Sometimes the lack of this information will cause the referral process to break down even though other aspects of the intervention have been properly conducted.

m. Find out if the offices of the referral source have made provisions for persons with physical disabilities.

 n. Have your list of referral sources available for use during an intervention.

 o. When you are making a referral, do the following:

  (1) Print the information about the referral source on a card or piece of paper for the victim.

  (2) Carefully review the information with the victim.

  (3) In a telephone intervention, give the referral information slowly, clearly, and concisely. Ask the victim to repeat the information you have given and to write down the information if possible.

  (4) If you feel it might be helpful, help the victim make contact with the referral agency. For example, place the call to the agency from your office.

  (5) Double-check the accuracy of the referral information you provide to the victim or the family.

  (6) Ask the victim if the information is clear and understandable.

  (7) Ask victims if they know of any circumstance that would prevent their making contact with the referral agency or keeping an appointment with the agency.

  (8) If problems are identified, attempt to deal with them on the spot.

VI. Follow up with victims to ensure that they made contact with the referral agency.

 a. If the victim has not made contact with the referral agency within a reasonable amount of time, try to find out why.

 b. If necessary, attempt to help victims deal with their reasons for not contacting the referral agency.

 c. Re-refer victims as appropriate.

The following are explanations for each category on the American Academy of Crisis Interveners Lethality Scale and the Life Change Index Scale.

Age: Self-explanatory

Stress: At what level is the victim experiencing stress?

Resources: Personal, family, and social support available

Marital status: Self-explanatory

Psychological functioning: Person's functioning before this
 event

Symptoms: Self-explanatory

Communications: General level of interpersonal inter-
 action

Physical condition: Self-explanatory

Suicide by close family member: History of suicide in immediate family

Depressed/agitated: Self-explanatory

Prior suicidal behavior: History of attempts

Reaction by significant others: Self-explanatory

Financial stress: Self-explanatory

Suicidal plan: Current plan and specificity

Occupation: Self-explanatory

Residence: Self-explanatory

Living arrangements: Self-explanatory

Time of year: Current time of year

Day of week: Day of week crisis is occurring

Serious arguments with spouse: Self-explanatory

Significant other: Someone close to the victim who has
 disappointed or been lost to the victim through death,
 desertion, or divorce

AMERICAN ACADEMY OF
CRISIS INTERVENERS LETHALITY SCALE

Date _____

Name _____

	Criteria:	Minimal risk	(0–15)	____
		Low risk	(16–30)	____
		Medium risk	(31–46)	____
		High risk	(47–60)	____

(Continued)

Circle response in appropriate row and column and place score from top column in extreme right column. Sum all scores and match total with criteria.

	0	1	2	3	4	Score
Age Male	0–12		13–44	45–64	65 +	
Female	0–12	13–44	45 +			
Stress	Low		Medium		High	
Resources	Good	Fair		Poor		
Marital Status	Married with children	Married without children		Widowed Single	Divorced	
Psychological Functioning	Stable			Unstable		
Symptoms (alcoholism, drug addiction, homosexuality)	Absent			Present		
Communications	Open			Blocked		
Physical Condition	Good	Fair			Poor	
Suicide by Close Family Member	No		Yes			
Depressed/ Agitated	No				Yes	
Prior Suicidal Behavior	No		Yes			
Reaction by Significant Others	Helpful			Not helpful		
Financial Stress	Absent		Present			
Suicidal Plan	None	Few details	Means selected		Highly specific plan	
Occupation	Non-helping profession Other occupation	M.D. Dentist Attorney Helping profession	Psychiatrist Police officer Unemployed			
Residence	Rural	Suburban	Urban			
Living Arrangements	With others				Alone	
Time of Year		Spring				
Day of Week		Sunday Wednesday	Monday			
Serious Arguments with Spouse	No	Yes				
Significant Other (Recently)		Focus of disappointment	Loss of			

Intervener _____   Total _____

Reprinted with permission of A.A.C.I.

LIFE CHANGE INDEX SCALE

Look over the events listed in the Life Change Index Scale. Place a check (√) in the space next to a given event if it has happened to you within the last twelve months.

1. Death of spouse	1. _____	100
2. Divorce	2. _____	73
3. Marital separation from mate	3. _____	65
4. Detention in jail or other institution	4. _____	63
5. Death of a close family member	5. _____	63
6. Major personal injury or illness	6. _____	53
7. Marriage	7. _____	50
8. Being fired at work	8. _____	47
9. Marital reconciliation	9. _____	45
10. Retirement from work	10. _____	45
11. Major change in the health or behavior of a family member	11. _____	44
12. Pregnancy	12. _____	40
13. Sexual difficulties	13. _____	39
14. Gaining a new family member (e.g., through birth, adoption, oldster moving in, etc.)	14. _____	39
15. Major business readjustment (e.g., merger, reorganization, bankruptcy, etc.)	15. _____	38
16. Major change in financial state (e.g., either a lot worse off or a lot better off than usual)	16. _____	37
17. Death of a close friend	17. _____	36
18. Changing to a different line of work	18. _____	36
19. Major change in the number of arguments with spouse (e.g., either a lot more or a lot less than usual regarding child-rearing, personal habits, etc.)	19. _____	35
20. Taking on a mortgage greater than $10,000 (e.g., purchasing a home, business, etc.)	20. _____	31
21. Foreclosure on a mortgage or loan	21. _____	30
22. Major change in responsibilities at work (e.g., promotion, demotion, lateral transfer)	22. _____	29
23. Son or daughter leaving home (e.g., marriage, attending college, etc.)	23. _____	29
24. In-law troubles	24. _____	29
25. Outstanding personal achievement	25. _____	28
26. Spouse beginning or ceasing work outside the home	26. _____	26
27. Beginning or ceasing formal schooling	27. _____	26

(Continued)

28. Major change in living conditions (e.g. building a new home, remodeling, deterioration of home or neighborhood)   28. _____   25
29. Revision of personal habits (dress, manners, associations, etc.)   29. _____   24
30. Troubles with the boss   30. _____   23
31. Major change in working hours or conditions   31. _____   20
32. Change in residence   32. _____   20
33. Changing to a new school   33. _____   20
34. Major change in usual type and/or amount of recreation   34. _____   19
35. Major change in church activities (e.g., a lot more or a lot less than usual)   35. _____   19
36. Major change in social activities (e.g., clubs, dancing, movies, visiting, etc.)   36. _____   18
37. Taking on a mortgage or loan less than $10,000 (e.g., purchasing a car, TV, freezer, etc.)   37. _____   17
38. Major change in sleeping habits (a lot more or a lot less sleep or change in time of day when asleep)   38. _____   16
39. Major change in number of family get-togethers (e.g., a lot more or a lot less than usual)   39. _____   15
40. Major change in eating habits (a lot more or a lot less food intake, or very different meal hours or surroundings)   40. _____   15
41. Vacation   41. _____   13
42. Christmas   42. _____   12
43. Minor violations of the law (e.g., traffic tickets, jaywalking, disturbing the peace, etc.)   43. _____   11

From "The Holmes and Rahe Social Readjustment Rating Scale" by T. Holmes and Rahe in the *Journal of Psychosomatic Research, 11,* 213–218, 1967. Copyright © 1967 by Pergamon Press. Reprinted by permission.

Scoring the Scale

Add the number of points next to each of your check marks. Place the total in the box below.

Total Life Change Units (LCU)

Interpreting Your Score

Dr. Holmes and his colleagues have clearly shown the relationship between recent life changes and future illness. Listed below are the score categories and the associated probability of illness during the next two years for a person with that score.

0–150	No significant problem
150–199	Mild Life Crisis Level with a 35 percent chance of illness
200–299	Moderate Life Crisis Level with a 50 percent chance of illness
300 or over	Major Life Crisis Level with an 80 percent chance of illness

It is not only your life change unit (LCU) total score that is related to your likelihood of illness. Also important with your amount of change is how you respond to those changes. Psychologists have found that when they match two groups, both with LCU totals over 300, those who developed physical illnesses had more difficulty in coping emotionally with life changes than those who did not get sick. Aspects of how you go through your daily life, such as feeling the need to get everything done right on time, also are involved in how you handle potentially troublesome levels of life changes.

This means that after you total your LCUs, you also need to think about how emotionally strong you are to handle those changes and how good your present techniques are for relaxing and easing the pressure.

Your own LCU may suggest a higher—or lower— probability of illness depending on how you deal with stress as it arises. Just being aware of the concept of stress and how life changes increase stress can reduce your own likelihood of getting ill. You can reduce the stress of adjusting to change even further by developing specific techniques, such as relaxation, hobbies, exercise, and meditation.

About the Scale

The most common stress-producing situations in modern life involve fear and frustration. Most people would agree that there is a high degree of stress involved in negative events related to these two emotions, events such as death of a spouse, marital separation, or going to jail. But it took a group of researchers at the University of Washington School of Medicine to point out and quantify that *any* major life change, even a positive one, produces stress. The research team, led by Dr. Thomas Holmes, found in a group of 400 people a high relationship between their amount of life changes during the previous six months and their likelihood of getting sick.

Out of such research came the Life Change Index Scale which rates 43 life events on the degree of stress each produces. The subsequent research needed to validate the scale is fascinating. The study mentioned earlier involved having 400 people count their *life change units* (LCU) over a six-month and one-year period with the researcher then predicting, on the basis of LCU totals, which people would develop a major health problem during the next six months. Another study measured LCU totals in a group of 2684 Navy and Marine personnel getting ready for a six-month cruise and predicted which people would need the most visits to sick bay during the cruise. Yet another research project involved the prediction of football injuries during a season on the basis of LCU totals for team members before the season began. In each of these studies, plus numerous others, life change unit totals were highly related to the likelihood of any specific person developing a major health problem.

As you look over the events, you will notice that an event such as marital separation produces more stress than a personal illness or injury. But the positive change of getting back together, marital reconciliation, produces more stress than a situation involving sex difficulties. Dr. Holmes and his colleagues were among the first researchers to quantify what stress expert Dr. Hans Selye had said for several years, that we must watch out for the impact of positive life changes as well as those that are clearly negative. As Drs. Holmes and Masuda wrote, "If it takes too much effort to cope with the environment, we have less to spare for preventing disease. When life is too hectic and when coping attempts fail, illness is the unhappy result."

CHAPTER THREE

A POTPOURRI OF MISTAKEN ASSUMPTIONS

"IF YOU CAN'T HELP THEM, AT LEAST DON'T HURT THEM."

The assumption here is that there can be a "noneffect" of intervention on the sufferer. This is not so. When one intervenes in another person's crisis, that person will either be helped or hurt as a result of the intervention. Under no circumstances will the sufferer be unaffected. The effect, whether positive or negative, will be determined by what the intervener does or does not do. Therefore, knowing when to stay out is as important as knowing when to become involved. There is no shame in not intervening if you decide that your skills are inadequate in a particular situation or that your own psychological well-being is at stake. However, if you decide to intervene in a situation that you cannot handle, your involvement will worsen the situation. Your decision to intervene requires you to accept that your action will have some direct, important impact on the person in crisis.

"I KNOW EXACTLY HOW YOU FEEL."

Even under the best conditions, this is doubtful. If you say you know and you really do not, your credibility as an intervener is destroyed. If you make such a statement to a victim, be prepared to back it up with accurate information about the sufferer's feelings. Making assumptions about the sufferer's feelings too early in the intervention can prove disastrous. Victims of a crisis often want to talk to someone, but they will not talk indiscriminately. Being in crisis does not preclude testing the sincerity of those who say they want to help. The victim can challenge your assumption by saying, "OK, how do I feel?" or "How can you know how I feel? We just met!" The unprepared intervener may have to do some fast backpedaling.

"IF I ASK ABOUT SUICIDE, THE PERSON MIGHT DO IT."

Wrong again! The victim from whom you receive signals about suicide is already considering it. In fact, even if the person is not considering suicide, the fact that you are open about the subject may make it easier to talk about in the future. Almost all of us have at least had passing thoughts about what suicide is or how it could affect us. For the sufferer contemplating a suicidal act, your use of the term *suicide* may make it less frightening and therefore easier to talk about. If you are not afraid to use the term, maybe the sufferer does not have to be uncomfortable with it either. Be assured that using the terms *suicide* or *killing yourself* will not cause the act to happen.

"I CAN RELAX AFTER THE PARTIES ARE SEATED."

Never relax during an intervention!! Although it is true that it is harder to remain physically aggressive while seated, never underestimate your situation or its potential for violence. An eruption can occur at any time and can affect you directly and severely. Having to be "on your toes" all the time is a major reason that Crisis Intervention can be physically and emotionally exhausting to the intervener as well as to the victim. Not everyone can perform Crisis Intervention effectively. However, if you are going to intervene effectively, be prepared for the drain on your energy and stamina.

"LISTENING TO AND ACKNOWLEDGING FEELINGS IMPLIES THAT I AGREE WITH THE VICTIM AND THE VICTIM'S BEHAVIOR."

Relationships are not built on agreement; they are built on understanding. Serious disagreements can exist within a close personal relationship if both parties know that each will take the time to understand the other. Similarly, with a person in crisis, it is possible to listen and respond to feelings even though you may not agree with the person's actions. In fact, sometimes you may need to tell the person about your non-agreement. This honesty will not interfere with the relationship-building necessary to the intervention or subsequent referral. Rather, the intervention may gain even greater strength because of your ability to differentiate between feelings and agreement. Also, remember that victims' asking for agreement with their actions may be a way of testing the intervener's sincerity and honesty. The intervener's credibility is at issue here.

"MY DEGREE, BADGE, OR PROFESSION WILL AUTOMATICALLY MAKE ME AN EFFECTIVE INTERVENER."

Unfortunately, this has long been thought to be the case. It was often assumed that if you were a good therapist, for example, that you were also a qualified crisis intervener. The results of this mistaken belief have often been very bad, to say the least. Practice has demonstrated repeatedly that one must learn and apply Crisis Intervention skills as a separate discipline rather than as the stepchild of some other part of the behavioral sciences. Although psychologists, counselors, mediators, psychiatrists, or social workers may make excellent crisis interveners in many settings, the fact that one has such a title does not in itself ensure skilled crisis management. Often, those most skilled in Crisis Intervention have not been trained in any of the behavioral science disciplines. Professional training may make us skilled professionals in our field, but it may not qualify us to apply what we know in ways specific to Crisis Intervention.

CHAPTER FOUR

SPECIAL ISSUES

SAFETY FOR THE INTERVENER

During an intervention, the crisis intervener's safety is a major consideration. The possibility of injury to the intervener exists regardless of professional capacity. For that reason, we suggest the following safety procedures. The procedures must be adapted to each individual crisis situation and to the intervener's skill and training.

Out of the Office

1. If possible, always intervene with a partner. This is especially important when there is more than one victim or disputant.
2. Approach the crisis or potential crisis slowly and carefully. If approaching a house, building, or room, take time to survey the surroundings for clues that might help later. Although time is critical in Crisis Intervention, the precautions you take at the outset may prevent problems later.

3. If you are in a car, do not park directly in front of the area where the crisis is occurring. Assess what is happening around you as you leave your vehicle. Be observant at all times.

4. Approach all doors or openings with caution. Do not stand directly in front of doors or windows. Stand to one side, and only then, knock on the door. Interveners have been killed or injured during family disputes by bullets fired through a door in response to the intervener's knock.

5. Before knocking or ringing the doorbell, listen for 10 to 15 seconds for additional clues that may be helpful to you as you enter the situation. These may include screaming, objects being broken, weapons being fired, angry voices, or threats. Perhaps you will hear no noise at all.

6. Once the door is opened, maintain control of the situation by keeping everyone involved in front of you and within eyesight.

7. Perform a visual "frisk" of all persons in the room to determine if weapons are hidden in pockets, belts, shoes, and so on. Pay attention!!

8. Observe the persons in crisis. What are they doing? What must you do immediately to stabilize the situation? Do it!

9. Note any objects in the room that could be used in a violent way. A heavy ashtray or an innocent letter opener could become a lethal weapon in the hands of a violent person.

10. Be aware of all other persons in the room, and note all persons who enter after you arrive. Assume nothing. Observe both the verbal and nonverbal behavior of everyone in the room. Find out who else is in the house and their location, if possible.

11. Be prepared for unexpected behavior of significant others, neighbors, or visitors in the house.

12. Initially, step into the room only a few feet at a time. Proceed only as far as it seems safe.

13. If necessary, separate the disputants. Avoid using the kitchen or bedroom; weapons are often stored in those areas.

14. Gain control as quickly as possible. You may use anything short of physical force, as appropriate and according to your training. A shrill whistle, a loud clap, a loud voice, an absurd request under the circumstances (asking permission to use a phone book, for example), or other attention-getting device may be used for this purpose.

15. Have the victims sit down. The failure of disputants to sit does not preclude a successful intervention. However, the potential for violence and aggression seems to be lower when everyone is seated.

16. Select an appropriate place to sit so you can maintain your own safety, gain and maintain control of the situation, and proceed with the intervention.

17. Visually assess the room and the adjoining areas, if possible.

18. Know where entrances and exits are.

19. Know where you might get assistance should you need it. Is there a working telephone in the room? Do you have a portable phone or radio?

20. Sit in the following manner: feet solidly on the floor with heels and toes touching the floor; hands unfolded in your lap; your body leaning slightly forward toward the victim. This position accomplishes two important functions:

    a. It gives the victim the feeling that you are attentive to what is being said and experienced. Your body language conveys a sense of interest and concern.

    b. It permits you to respond immediately should you be physically threatened. Although a crossed-leg, folded-arm position, or a similarly relaxed position, may be more comfortable, it can reduce your ability to respond quickly should an immediate response be needed.

21. Attempt to speak with the crisis victim at eye level.
22. Avoid standing above the victim in an authoritarian or parental manner. If the victim chooses to remain standing, you should remain standing also.
23. Do not turn your back on a crisis victim or allow the victim to walk behind you.
24. Do not position yourself in a corner from which you cannot exit if necessary.
25. Remove any objects or extraneous clothing parts that a violent victim could use against you. Name tags connected by pins; pens and pencils; regular, non–clip-on neckties; scarves; and jewelry, such as chain necklaces or hoop earrings, are all potential weapons in the wrong hands.
26. Stand in the following manner: feet placed shoulder-width apart; one foot slightly behind the other; weight on the rear leg; knees slightly bent; hands folded, but not interlocked, on the upper abdomen or lower chest; arms unfolded. This unrestricted stance permits instant response to a physical threat. Hands placed in one's pockets are suspect, and having to remove your hands from your pockets increases your response time. Folded arms can be threatening and can also impede your response. Maintaining your weight on the rear leg with knees slightly bent permits quick movement in almost any direction without affecting balance.
27. Once separated, bring the disputants back together as soon as it seems productive to do so.
28. Maintain eye contact with your partner and attempt to break eye contact between the disputants as soon as possible.

In the Office

1. In the office, allow for maximum personal safety by doing the following:

    a. Remove potential weapons such as heavy ashtrays, paperweights, letter openers, scissors, and the like.

    b. Arrange seating so that victims have access to the exit without going over you.

    c. When you greet victims, notice anything strange or unusual about their words, actions, or dress. Allow your senses to give you clues, and take all clues seriously until you have been able to rule them out.

    d. Read the victims' body language as they enter.

    e. Enter the room behind the victims. Visually "frisk" the victims.

    f. If possible, arrange several seating areas within the room that can be used as needed with different threat levels.

    g. Do not remain after hours with a potentially violent victim unless proper security is available.

    h. Arrange a "buddy system" so that someone is available should you need help.

    i. If you know that the victims are involved in situations where there is a potential for violence, arrange to have a co-intervener in the office with you, or at least close at hand. As appropriate, inform the victim about other persons available.

    j. After hours, enter your office in the same careful manner that you would enter a crisis victim's house.

    k. Enter elevators only after checking for other passengers.

    l. Know your emergency telephone numbers and use them if you need help. Do not hesitate.

2. If at all possible, always intervene with a partner.
3. Make contingency plans for all interventions. Consider what you would do under a variety of conditions. Learn to play the "what if" game. Play it

often. Preplanning will affect automatic behavior under stress.

4. Always take safety precautions seriously. The intervention and your life may depend on your behavior in this regard.

GUIDELINES FOR INCREASING THE CRISIS INTERVENER'S MULTICULTURAL AWARENESS

1. Attempt to become aware of your own cultural biases.
2. If possible, learn the language of those into whose crisis you may need to intervene. Find a qualified translator if necessary.
3. Ask for clarification if you are not sure what the victim said.
4. Do not assume that you understand any nonverbal communication unless you are familiar with the victim's culture.
5. Do not impose your personal values.
6. If the victim's nonverbal communication is insulting in your culture, do not take it personally.
7. Develop an awareness of anything in your own nonverbal communication that might be insulting in certain cultures.
8. Make every effort to increase your awareness of your own preconceptions and stereotypes of the cultures you may encounter.
9. With your increased awareness, reinterpret the behavior of people from another culture from *their* cultural perspective.
10. Be willing to test, adapt, and change your perceptions to fit your new experience.
11. Maintain objectivity.
12. Recognize that you cannot change a person's cultural perspectives.

13. Do not judge people from another culture by your own cultural values until you have come to know the people and their cultural values.
14. Recognize that lack of familiarity with a victim's culture may increase the stress within the intervention.
15. Clarify your role, knowledge, and experience with the parties so you maintain the integrity demanded by your position as intervener.

Partially adapted from *A Handbook for Developing Multicultural Awareness* (pp. 23–25) by P. A. Pederson, 1988, New York: American Association for Counseling and Development.

CHAPTER FIVE

INTERVENER SURVIVAL

High stress levels, personal frustration, and inadequate coping skills have major personal, organizational, and social costs. Stress is not a mental illness, but a part of everyday living. Each of us is potentially vulnerable to the problems of too much stress and too little coping ability.

SIGNS AND SYMPTOMS
OF STRESS AND BURNOUT

1. High resistance to going to work every day
2. A pervasive sense of failure, as indicated by such expressions as "I can't do enough"; "I can't get it right"; "I'm no good anymore."
3. Anger and resentment
4. Guilt and blame. These may be evidenced by such expressions as, "No matter how many hours I work, I never finish, and I feel guilty about leaving. I'm in a 'no-win' situation."
5. Discouragement and indifference

6. Negativism
7. Isolation and withdrawal
8. Feelings of tiredness and exhaustion that last all day
9. Frequent clock watching
10. Extreme fatigue after work
11. Loss of positive feelings toward victims
12. Postponement of victim contacts; resistance to client phone calls and office visits
13. Inability to concentrate or listen to information
14. Feelings of immobilization
15. Cynicism toward victims, co-workers, or the world in general
16. Sleep disorders, including difficulty either in falling asleep or in staying asleep, or sleeping an adequate amount but feeling unrested upon waking. These disorders occur regularly over an extended period
17. Self-preoccupation
18. Becoming more approving of behavior-control measures, such as tranquilizers
19. Frequent colds and flus
20. Frequent headaches and gastrointestinal disturbances
21. Rigidity in thinking and resistance to change
22. Suspicion and paranoia
23. Excessive drug use
24. Marital and family conflict
25. Free-floating anxiety, evidenced by such expressions as, "I'm constantly worried and anxious, but I can't pinpoint what I'm upset about. It just seems to hover there."
26. Tunnel vision: as stress increases, perception of available options narrows
27. A sense of increasing helplessness
28. Fear that "it won't get better"
29. Fear of losing control
30. High absenteeism

Intervener and victim alike are subject to stressors, and both can become incapacitated as a result of unmanaged stress.

A person in crisis cannot assist another person who is also in crisis.

ENSURING INTERVENER SURVIVAL

Intervener survival addresses the needs and concerns of the intervener in preparation for, or in the actual performance of, intervention in a crisis. It is not sufficient to learn crisis management procedures without attending to the sources of stress and tension that could impinge on the intervener. Such tension can affect the intervener's ability to intervene effectively and efficiently. Interveners who experience a personal crisis while trying to help others who are also in crisis are of no help to anyone, least of all themselves.

In intervening in the crises of others, the intervener may neglect personal needs, health and nutrition, personal safety, and responsibility for self-direction. Interveners may become so involved in others' lives that they forget to pay attention to themselves. Continually discounting personal needs, or failing to value oneself as one values those being helped, can interfere with effectiveness. Additionally, the intervener could experience physical and emotional harm. If interveners neglect concern for personal safety during interventions or fail to recognize that they are experiencing stress, productivity and efficiency will suffer.

Conversely, if interveners are aware of these areas and have spent the time and energy needed to attend to them, they will be better prepared to focus on the crises of others. Regardless of the intervener's attempt to disavow ownership for feelings of frustration, anger, stress, and tension, these feelings and the resulting behavior remain a personal responsibility.

The following are suggestions for keeping stress within tolerable limits:

1. Eliminate stressor foods from your diet. Nutritional stress can be as debilitating as emotional stress.
2. Get enough rest and sleep.

3. Exercise regularly and appropriately for your age and fitness level.

4. Be realistic about the givens of your world. Work within the reality of "what is" today.

5. Realistically assess what you are able to do in your particular situation.

6. Schedule time for fun. Allow time each day to experience good feelings.

7. Schedule time each week for dreaming, thinking, wandering, exploring, planning, and being in touch with your dreams.

8. Schedule regular recreation or vacation time. The quantity of time spent is not important; the quality of time spent in recreation is the key to stress reduction.

9. Be sure you get your minimum daily requirement of positive "strokes."

10. Set realistic goals in all areas of your life.

11. Consider the following carefully:

    a. Everything I do is the result of a choice I make.

    b. Every choice I make benefits me positively in some way, even though I may not know what the benefit is at the moment.

    c. I have inside me everything I need and all the tools I need to guide my life successfully.

    d. I can choose to gain greater self-awareness.

    e. I am responsible for 100 percent of my life.

    f. The degree to which others control my life is the degree to which I allow them to control it.

    g. I cannot voluntarily change my feelings, but I can always voluntarily change my behavior.

    h. Any problem I experience in my life is a problem I have created for myself.

    i. If I choose to continue creating a particular problem for myself, I do it because
        (1) I receive some pleasure or unacknowledged benefit or payoff for continuing the problem, or

(2) I can avoid a greater or more fearful problem by perpetuating the current problem. In other words, if I solve the current problem, I am afraid the greater problem will occur.

CHAPTER SIX

CHILDREN'S REACTION TO CRISIS

TIPS FOR TEACHERS IN TIMES OF CRISIS

Taking Care of Yourself and Other School Staff

As teachers or school personnel, you are often in the "front lines" when dealing with children's reactions to crisis. You also need to consider your own crisis-related stress. It is extremely important to recognize that you, too, are under particular stress and vulnerable to "burnout."

Burnout reactions include the following:

- Depression, irritability, anxiety, overexcitability, excessive rage, and other similar reactions
- Physical exhaustion, loss of energy, gastrointestinal distress, appetite disturbances, hypochondria, sleep disorders, and tremors
- Hyperactivity, excessive fatigue, inability to express yourself verbally or in writing

- Slowness of thought, inability to make decisions, loss of objectivity in evaluating your own functioning, and external confusion

It is important to recognize the symptoms and find ways to relieve the stress. You and others around you can form a support system by allowing each person to vent his or her experiences. Time might be set aside in staff meetings to discuss your own responses to the crisis as well as to share ideas on dealing with and assisting students.

Teaching is a highly stressful job under the best of circumstances. Dealing with your own responses to a crisis in addition to your students' reactions could easily feel overwhelming at times. Recognizing this fact and taking care of yourself and other school staff can help keep the stress at a manageable level.

GENERAL REACTIONS OF CHILDREN TO CRISIS

Although many feelings and reactions are shared by people of all ages in response to the direct or indirect effects of crisis, meeting the needs of children requires special attention.

Typical reactions of children, regardless of age, include the following:

- Fears stemming from the crisis extending to their home or neighborhood
- Loss of interest in school
- Regressive behavior
- Sleep disturbances and night terrors
- Fears of events that may be associated with the crisis situation, such as airplane sounds or loud noises

REACTIONS OF SPECIFIC AGE GROUPS

Children of different age groups tend to react in unique ways to the stress caused by crises and their consequences. The following typical reactions to stress are summarized for each age group and are followed by suggested responses.

Preschool (Ages 1 through 5)

Typical reactions to stress include the following:

- thumb-sucking
- bed-wetting
- fear of the dark or of animals
- clinging to parents
- night terrors
- loss of bladder or bowel control or constipation
- speech difficulties
- loss of or increase in appetite
- fear of being left alone
- immobility

Children in this age group are particularly vulnerable to disruption of their previously secure world. Because they lack the verbal and conceptual skills necessary to cope effectively with sudden stress by themselves, they look to family members for comfort. These children are often strongly affected by the reactions of parents and other family members.

Abandonment is a major fear in this age group. Children who have lost family members (or even pets or toys) due to circumstances either related or unrelated to the crisis will need special reassurance.

The goal of the following responses is to help children integrate their experiences and reestablish a sense of security and mastery:

- Encourage expression through play reenactment where appropriate.
- Provide verbal reassurance and physical comforting.
- Give the child frequent attention.
- Encourage the child's expression of feelings and concerns regarding the loss, temporary or permanent, of family members, pets, toys, or friends.
- Provide comforting bedtime routines.

- Allow the child to sleep in the same room with the parent. Make it clear to the child that this is only for a limited period.

Early Childhood (Ages 5 through 11)

Common reactions to stress in this age group include the following:

- irritability
- whining
- clinging
- aggressive behavior at home or at school
- overt competition with younger siblings for parent's attention
- night terrors, nightmares, or fear of darkness
- school avoidance
- loss of interest and poor concentration in school
- fear of personal harm
- confusion
- fear of abandonment
- generalized anxiety

Fear of loss is particularly difficult for these children to handle, and regressive behavior is most typical of this age group.

The following responses may be helpful:

- Patience and tolerance.
- Play sessions with adults and peers where affective reactions can be openly discussed.
- Discussions with adults and peers about frightening, anxiety-producing aspects of events and about appropriate behavior to manage the child's concerns and the stress.
- Relaxation of expectations at school or at home. It should be made clear to the child that this relaxation is temporary and that the normal routine will be resumed after a suitable period.
- Opportunities for structured, but not unusually demanding, chores and responsibilities at home.

- Maintenance of a familiar routine as much as possible and as soon as possible.

Preadolescent (Ages 11 through 14)

The following are common reactions to stress for this age group:

- sleep disturbances
- appetite disturbance
- rebellion in the home
- refusal to do chores
- school problems, such as fighting, withdrawal, loss of interest, and attention-seeking behavior
- physical problems, such as headaches, vague aches and pains, skin eruptions, bowel problems, and psychosomatic complaints
- loss of interest in peer social activities
- fear of personal harm
- fear of impending loss of family members, friends, or home
- anger
- denial
- generalized anxiety

Peer reactions are especially significant in preadolescence. These children need to feel that their fears are both appropriate and shared by others. Responses should be aimed at lessening tensions, anxieties, and possible guilt feelings.

The following responses may be helpful for children in this age group:

- group activities geared toward the resumption of routines
- involvement with same-age group activity
- group discussions geared toward examining feelings about the crisis and appropriate behavior to manage the concerns and the stress
- structured, but undemanding, responsibilities
- temporarily relaxed expectations of performance at school and at home
- additional individual attention and consideration

Adolescent (Ages 14 through 18)

Common reactions in this age group include the following:

- psychosomatic symptoms, such as rashes, bowel problems, and asthma
- headaches and tension
- appetite and sleep disturbances
- hypochondriasis
- amenorrhea or dysmenorrhea
- agitation or decrease in energy level
- apathy
- decline in interest in the opposite sex
- irresponsible behavior, delinquent behavior, or both
- decline in emancipatory struggles over parental control
- poor concentration
- guilt
- fear of loss

Most of the activities and interests of adolescents are focused in their own age-group peers. Adolescents tend to be especially distressed by the disruption of their peer-group activities and by their lack of access to full adult responsibilities in community efforts.

We recommend the following responses:

- Encourage participation in the community and in individual responses, such as letter writing.
- Encourage discussion of feelings, concerns, and shared information with peers and extrafamily significant others.
- Temporarily reduce expectations for specific levels of both school and general performance, depending on individual reactions.
- Encourage, but do not insist upon, discussions of crisis-induced fears within the family setting.

WHEN TO REFER CHILDREN TO MENTAL HEALTH PROFESSIONALS

There is a wide range of normal reactions surrounding crisis. Usually the reactions can be dealt with by support at home and at school. This is not always the case, however. There may be times when a teacher needs to recommend professional help. In making such a referral, it is important to stress that it is not a sign of the parents' failure if they find they cannot help their child by themselves. It is also important to note that early action will help the child return to normal functioning and avoid more severe problems later.

Students who have lost family members or friends, either temporarily or permanently, or feel that they were in extreme danger, are at special risk. Those who have been involved in individual or family crises in addition to the crisis they are currently experiencing may have more difficulty dealing with the additional stress. Counseling may be recommended as a preventive measure when these circumstances are known to exist.

If symptoms that are considered normal reactions persist for several months; disrupt the student's social, mental, or physical functioning; or both, referral is recommended.

Referral for Preschool and Elementary School Children

Consider referring the family for professional help if the children

- seem excessively withdrawn and depressed
- do not respond to special attention and attempts to draw them out

Referral for Junior and Senior High School Children

Consider referral to a mental health professional if students

- are disoriented; for example, are unable to give their own name and address or the date
- complain of significant memory gaps
- are despondent and show agitation, restlessness, and pacing
- are severely depressed and withdrawn
- mutilate themselves
- use drugs or alcohol excessively

- are unable to care for themselves in such areas as eating, drinking, bathing, and dressing
- repeat ritualistic acts
- experience hallucinations, such as hearing voices or seeing visions
- state that their body feels "unreal" and express the concern that they are "going crazy"
- are excessively preoccupied with one idea or thought
- have the delusion that someone or something is out to get them and their family
- are afraid they will commit suicide or kill another person
- are unable to make simple decisions or carry out everyday functions
- show extremely pressured speech or talk overflow

CLASSROOM ACTIVITIES

Creative classroom activities may be helpful to teachers seeking ways to deal with the stress and tension a crisis and its consequences creates in students. The following activities are vehicles for expression and discussion for students and are important steps in helping children handle the stress they are experiencing. You can use these activities to stimulate your own ideas and adapt them to meet both your students' needs and your teaching style.

PRESCHOOL ACTIVITIES

1. Make available some toys that encourage play enactment of the child's concerns. Such toys might include airplanes, helicopters, toy police officers, toy soldiers, rescue trucks, ambulances, building blocks, puppets, or dolls. Playing with these toys allows the child to ventilate feelings about what is occurring or has already occurred.
2. Children need lots of physical contact during times of stress to help them reestablish ego boundaries and

a sense of security. Introduce games that involve physical toughening among children within a structure. Examples include "Ring around the Rosy," "London Bridge," and "Duck, Duck, Goose."

3. Provide extra amounts of drinks and finger foods in small portions. This is a concrete way of supplying the emotional and physical nourishment children need in times of stress. Oral satisfaction is especially necessary because children tend to revert to more regressive behavior in response to feeling that their survival or security is threatened.

4. Have the children make a mural on butcher paper, using topics related to what is happening in the world and in their community. This is recommended for small groups, with discussion afterwards facilitated by the teacher or other skilled adult.

5. Have the children draw individual pictures about the crisis situation and then discuss the pictures in small groups. This activity allows children to vent their experiences and to discover that others share their fears.

6. Make a group collage, and discuss what the collage represents, how it was made, and the feelings it evokes.

ELEMENTARY SCHOOL ACTIVITIES

1. For younger children, make toys available that encourage play to express concerns, fears, and observations. These toys might include ambulances, planes, tanks, helicopters, toy police officers, rescue vehicles, toy soldiers, building blocks, and dolls. Play with puppets can provide ways for older children, as well as younger children, to ventilate their feelings.

2. Help or encourage the children to develop skits or puppet shows about what happened during the crisis. Encourage them to include anything positive about the experience as well as frightening or disconcerting aspects.

3. Have the children create short stories about the crisis and how it was managed. These stories can be either written or dictated to an adult, depending on the age of the child.

4. Have the children draw pictures and discuss them in relation to the crisis. It is important that the group discussion end on a positive note if at all possible. Mastery and having a vehicle for expressing concerns are equally important.

5. Stimulate group discussion about crisis and its consequences by showing your own feelings or fears. It is very important to legitimize children's feelings and to help children feel less isolated. It is equally important to give them a sense of structure, balance, and control over their own activities and life.

6. Have the children brainstorm their own ways of handling their concerns. Encourage them to discuss the results with their parents.

7. Encourage class activities in which the children can organize and build projects, such as scrapbooks, to give them a sense of mastery and ability to organize what seems chaotic and confusing.

8. Encourage the children to talk about their own feelings about the crisis.

JUNIOR AND SENIOR HIGH SCHOOL ACTIVITIES

1. Conduct a group discussion of the students' experiences concerning the crisis situation and the events surrounding it. This is particularly important to adolescents because they need the opportunity to vent as well as to normalize the extreme emotions that arise for them. A good way to stimulate such a discussion is for you to share your personal reactions. The students may need considerable reassurance that even extreme emotions and ''crazy'' thoughts are normal under these circumstances. It is important to end such

discussions on a positive note. Such discussion is appropriate for any course of study because it can hasten a return to more normal functioning.

2. Conduct a class discussion or support a class project on how students might involve themselves in activities related to managing the crisis. This might include support groups, rallies, and assistance to family members. It is important to help students develop concrete, realistic ways to assist or to be involved. This helps them to overcome the feelings of helplessness, frustration, and guilt common to these situations.

3. Introduce classroom activities that relate the crisis and its consequences to course study. This can be an effective way to help students integrate their own experiences or observations while providing specific learning experiences. In performing these activities, it is very important to allow time for the students to discuss feelings stimulated by the projects or the issues covered.

The following suggestions could be carried out within specific courses. Teachers are encouraged to expand these suggestions to fit the students' needs and the teacher's individual style.

Journalism

Have the students write stories that cover different aspects of the crisis. These might include stories about community and personal impact, human interest, and ecological impact. You might also discuss issues such as accurate reporting, censorship, and sensationalism, and students could compile the stories into a special publication.

Science

Discuss the scientific aspects of the crisis, such as weapons and their destructive power, research, impact of the weather, environmental impact, and impact on the school. Suggest a project about stress involving the physiological responses to stress and methods of dealing with it.

English Composition

Have the students write about their own experiences, or those of persons close to them, regarding the crisis and the problems associated with it. You might discuss composition issues, such as the problems that arise in conveying heavy emotional tone without being overly dramatic.

Literature

Have students report on crises that have occurred in mythology or that appear in American and British fiction and poetry.

Psychology

Have the students apply what they have learned in the course to the emotions, behaviors, and stress reactions they felt or observed in response to the crisis. Cover posttraumatic stress syndrome as appropriate. Present a guest speaker from the mental health profession who may be involved in working with families affected by the crisis or with support groups. Have students discuss, from their own experience, what has helped them most in dealing with crisis-related stress. Have the students develop a mental health education brochure in which they discuss emotional and behavioral reactions to crisis and the things that are helpful in coping. Have students conduct a survey among their parents and friends about how the crisis affected each of them and how they reacted psychologically.

Peer Counseling

Provide special information on common responses to the onset of the crisis and the consequences associated with it. Encourage the students to help each other integrate their own experiences.

Health

Discuss emotional reactions to crisis and the importance of taking care of one's own emotional and physical well-being. Discuss health implications of crisis, including food, water, physical and mental wounds, exposure to the elements, and other health precautions and safety measures. Discuss the effects of adrenaline on the body during stress and danger. A public health or mental health professional could be invited to speak to the class. Maintaining health, from the viewpoints of all those involved in or affected by the crisis, might be a valuable discussion topic.

Art

Have the students portray the crisis and their concerns about it in various art media. Students can do this individually or as a group.

Speech and Drama

Have the students portray the emotions, feelings, and stresses that have arisen in response to the crisis and the effects of the crisis on each of them. Ask students to develop a skit or play on some aspect of the crisis. Stage a debate about whether women or men are better prepared psychologically to handle the stress of a crisis such as the one the students experienced.

Mathematics

Have the class solve mathematical problems related to the impact of the crisis.

Civics and Government

Study governmental agencies responsible either directly or indirectly for causing or supporting the crisis and their response to the crisis. Discuss how these agencies work and the political implications and impact of each agency. Examine various community systems and how the stress of the crisis has affected them. Have the students invite a local government official to class to discuss how the crisis has affected the community. Encourage the students to become aware of current and pending legislation relating to the crisis, should such legislation exist, and the implications of this legislation on them and on their families.

History

Have the students report on crises that have occurred both around the world and in the geographical location of the current crisis. What lessons can and have been learned that could benefit us and our community in the future?

AGE-SPECIFIC REACTIONS OF CHILDREN AFFECTED BY CRISIS AND ITS CONSEQUENCES

Preschoolers	Elementary School Children	Preadolescents and Adolescents
Crying	Headaches/physical complaints	Headaches/physical complaints
Thumbsucking	Depression	Depression
Loss of bowel control	Fears about safety	Confusion
Fears of being left alone and of strangers	Confusion	Poor performance
Irritability	Inability to concentrate	Aggressive behavior
Confusion	Poor performance	Withdrawal
Clinging	Fighting	Isolation
Immobility	Withdrawal from peers	

AGE-SPECIFIC INTERVENTIONS FOR CHILDREN REACTING TO CRISIS

Preschoolers	Elementary School Children	Preadolescents/ Adolescents
Draw a picture	Draw a picture	Stories and essays
Tell a story	Tell a story	Books on effects of crisis
Coloring books	Books on effects of crisis	Create a play about the crisis
Books on effects of crisis	Create a game	School project/ natural sciences
Doll, toy play	Create a play	School project/ social sciences
Group games	School study project	School health project
Talks about safety	Materials about personal and family safety	Materials about personal and family safety and community protection

CHAPTER SEVEN

HOT-LINE WORKERS

The immediacy of crisis situations dictates the need for immediate service delivery. Hot-line services are as close as the telephone and are usually available twenty-four hours a day, seven days a week. As a rule, the caller can obtain assistance without the need for self-identification.

Hot-line work is difficult. It requires that the intervener compensate for inability to see the caller's appearance, behavior, and body language as the caller speaks or listens.

DO'S

DO establish a feeling of trust, support, and confidence.

DO allow the caller to speak freely and to ventilate feelings.

DO listen carefully, not only to what is being said, but also to what is not being said.

DO encourage callers to tell you what is troubling them.

DO accept callers' right to feel as they do. The way they see the world at this time in their life is real for them.

DO listen attentively and reflect feelings.

DO be honest. If you do not know an answer or cannot provide the information requested, say so.

DO ask for feedback to find out if you are on the right track.

DO be realistic.

DO ask what the caller is doing currently to manage the particular discomfort the caller is experiencing.

DO ask how the caller has managed traumatic events in the past.

DO help the caller draw from past successes in managing current personal crises.

DO be alert for opportunities to reinforce the caller's strengths and positive qualities.

DO build a sense of structure that the caller can relate to.

DO help callers identify areas in their personal life over which they can assert control. Stress the need to devote energy to these areas rather than to areas over which they have no control.

DO have updated, immediately available referral resources.

DO get in touch and stay in touch with yourself and what you, as the hot-line worker, are feeling.

DO separate your needs, concerns, and values from the caller's. Respond to what the caller needs.

DO debrief with a fellow hot-line worker as needed.

DO trust yourself to ask effective questions, to offer appropriate options, and to know when to stop.

DO remember that your job is to listen, empathize, and help set some sense of structure for the caller, who may feel out of control.

DO remember that hot-line work is stressful. Take time to care for yourself as you care for others.

DON'TS

DON'T offer any service you cannot provide.

DON'T agree or disagree with callers. The way they see the world at this time is real to them.

DON'T interrupt callers while they are talking unless absolutely necessary. If you need more details, wait until the caller is finished, and then go back and ask for the needed information.

DON'T argue with a caller.

DON'T be afraid of silence. Give the caller time to think and feel.

DON'T assume anything. Ask for clarification if you are concerned about the caller's physical and emotional safety.

DON'T allow the caller's anger or hostility to intimidate you.

DON'T push your value system on the caller.

DON'T push your religious beliefs on the caller.

DON'T be afraid to admit that a caller might need further help that you cannot provide. Refer as necessary and as appropriate.

DON'T allow callers to concentrate only on the negative aspects of their situation. Help them develop options.

DON'T show excessive pity or sympathy.

TWENTY STEPS FOR HANDLING THE DIFFICULT CALLER

As hot-line workers and phone counselors, our job is to assist, to answer, perhaps to counsel, and certainly to help those who call. Occasionally the caller is upset to the point of belligerency either because of the emotional trauma suffered or because of extreme anger experienced for some other reason. Callers in this situation may become abusive to the hot-line worker and, if not checked appropriately, will contaminate all attempts to be helpful.

The following are suggested as a nonexhaustive guide to handling difficult and abusive calls and callers.

1. Stop talking.
2. Take a deep breath.
3. Listen for the caller's real message.

4. If possible, legitimize the caller's anger.
5. Listen carefully for clues as to what is really going on with the caller.
6. Reduce the volume of your own voice when speaking. This action on your part may cause the callers to lower their voice also, or at least to stop talking in order to hear what you are saying.
7. Do not argue with the caller or become defensive. The caller's remarks or abuse is usually not intended for you personally. The caller would probably make the same remarks to whomever answered the phone.
8. Clarify your role with the caller.
9. Refuse to be verbally abused by the caller. "I want to listen to what you are saying, but I won't listen to insults, threats, or personal attacks on me."
10. State the ground rules for your being able to provide assistance to the caller. These would include the caller's refraining from abusive talk.
11. Keep your responses clear and simple.
12. Once you have stated the ground rules, let the caller decide whether or not he or she wishes to continue the conversation. Continue with the conversation only if the caller agrees to abide by the ground rules.
13. Avoid being judgmental of anything the caller says. Remember, the way the caller sees the world is accurate for that caller.
14. Remember: Do not take personally any abusive remarks the caller makes to you.
15. Ask for and obtain a clear commitment from the caller that he or she will continue the conversation without abusive talk and according to the agreed-upon ground rules.
16. Continue to repeat your willingness to keep trying to assist the caller, and repeat the ground rules for continuing.
17. Always be aware of, and continue to evaluate, the caller's actual threat potential to you.

18. If all else fails in your attempt to deal with the caller's abusive or otherwise difficult behavior, terminate the call.
19. Debrief immediately after a difficult or abusive phone call.
20. *Remember: You are the professional, and you are in Control.*

CHAPTER EIGHT

FAMILY CRISIS

Excessive stress and tension, usually resulting from multiple or major changes in a person's life, are often the basis of most crisis situations. Because family members do not operate in a vacuum, one person's crisis often becomes a crisis for the family. Major sources of personal crises include illness, financial problems, business problems, job promotions or demotions, problems with one's children, layoffs, maintenance of a career or the beginning of a new one, adoption or birth of children, abortion, pending marriages, separations and divorces, blending of stepfamilies, and severe injuries and deaths in the family. These events can also be a source of crisis for all the members of a family.

Most crises have a primary victim, but they also touch those who are affected through the primary victim. These secondary victims are usually significant others of the person experiencing the crisis. In rapes, suicide, battering, incest, drug abuse, family disputes, and natural disasters, the intensity of the trauma, the emotional upheaval, and the difficulty in adjustment relating to the event may be as severe for the significant others as for the primary victim. Secondary victims often experience their own crisis as they try to fit what has happened into life as they see it. For example, a rape victim's parents, spouse, or boyfriend, or the children who may have witnessed the rape, may experience their own crisis with an intensity equal to, or even greater than, that of the primary victim. Guidelines and procedures for managing crisis situations with primary victims must be applied in a similar manner to significant others. Unfortunately, the intervener often overlooks this task.

Children may have it worst of all. Generally they lack even the limited understanding adults possess. Children's reality is often formed by fantasy, partial truths, and an immature ability to discern what is happening around them.

THIRTY STEPS FOR HANDLING FAMILY CRISES

1. Pull together as a family by establishing a sense of purpose.
2. Allow your feelings to be whatever they are; avoid berating yourself or discounting your feelings or those of your children.
3. Let your children talk with you about their fears, concerns, confusion, anger, sadness, and problems.
4. Talk in words your children can understand. Avoid euphemisms.
5. Allow your children to see your grief, and be honest with them about your feelings. Avoid as much gore as possible in your expressions.
6. Don't expect your children to resolve your grief.
7. Reassure children that they are safe and will be taken care of.
8. Don't be afraid to say that you do not know the answers to your children's questions. Your honesty may make it easier for them to tolerate the ambiguity in their own mind.

9. If a death occurs, share with your children in terms that they can understand, and avoid euphemisms. Straight talk usually works best.

10. Remember that children often take their lead as to their own behavior from their parents. They will watch and learn how you handle crises.

11. Children will look to you for structure, guidance, limits, and support. Give these things to them.

12. Ask your children what they need from you. Maybe they need a hug, time to talk, play time with you, or straight talk. Children of different ages will need different things at different times. Adapt your actions to your children's ages and levels of maturity.

13. Identify areas of concern in your life over which you have control, and exercise that control.

14. Have realistic expectations of yourself and your children in order to minimize stress.

15. Be realistic about each child's role in the family.

16. Continue projects that you have already begun.

17. Create a routine for yourself, and stick with it.

18. Maintain your personal health and hygiene.

19. Plan outings and activities with friends. This mutual support can be helpful.

20. Set boundaries with your children. Hear their feelings, and understand the behavior that might result from these feelings. Establish limits to provide stability, structure, and continuity. Don't overdo it by being too strict or too lenient.

21. Observe changes in your children's behavior, attitudes, and expressions. Pay attention to both verbal and nonverbal behavior. Be prepared to respond as appropriate.

22. Use support groups as necessary for your children and for yourself. Participate separately or together with your children, as appropriate.

23. Obtain professional help for yourself and your children as needed. Sometimes counseling in conjunction with support groups offers maximum benefit.

24. Find something to laugh about every day. Use laughter as a stress manager and reducer.
25. Walk or exercise regularly, and include sufficient rest and relaxation in your schedule.
26. Both for yourself and for your children, maintain the continuity of the familiar. This includes schedules, school attendance, friendships, TV programs, and regular activities.
27. Listen.
28. Hear.
29. Respond.
30. Don't lecture.

HOW PARENTS CAN HELP THEIR CHILDREN COPE WITH CRISIS-RELATED FEELINGS

1. Talk with your child; provide simple, accurate answers to questions.
2. Talk with your child about your own feelings.
3. Listen to what your child says and how your child says it. Does the child display fear, anxiety, or insecurity? Your repeating the child's words can be very helpful. Use such phrases as "You are afraid that . . . " or "You wonder if. . . . " This helps both you and the child clarify feelings.
4. Reassure your child. For example, tell the child, "We are together. I care about you, and I will take care of you."
5. You may need to repeat information and reassurances to your child many times. Do not stop responding just because you told the child something once.
6. Hold your child. Provide comfort. Touching is important for children during crises.
7. Spend extra time putting your child to bed; talk and offer reassurance. Leave a night-light on if necessary.
8. Observe your child at play. Listen to what your child says, and watch how your child plays. Frequently

children express feelings of fear or anger while playing with dolls, toy trucks, or friends.

9. Provide play experiences to relieve tension. Work with
Play-Doh, paint pictures, play in water, and the like.
If children display a need to hit or kick, give them
something safe, such as a pillow or a ball.

10. If your child has an especially meaningful toy or
blanket, allow the child to rely on it somewhat more
than usual.

11. If you need professional assistance, seek it early to
maximize its benefits.

CRISIS, STRESS, AND HOLIDAY CELEBRATIONS

Thanksgiving, Christmas, Easter, Hanukkah, Passover, New
Year's Day, birthdays, and anniversaries all come sooner than
we expect. For many people, the prospect of the holidays and
of family celebrations is filled with anguish and anxiety. And
when these holidays and celebrations take place without that
special loved one, they are much harder to get through.
Holidays may be accompanied by the emotional battering of
anticipatory stress followed by postholiday blues. It can take
weeks to recover from the agony of unfulfilled expectations,
the debt resulting from overspending to create the "perfect
holiday," and the disappointment of rediscovering that family
conflicts and losses remain unresolved despite the promises
of holiday music and commercial messages.

Therapists know that holidays are times when patients
and clients often turn away from the hard work they have
been doing with their counselors and rely on the season, the
holiday, or the celebration to do it for them. Loan officers
know they will be deluged with requests from people who
will "buy now and worry later."

During holiday seasons loneliness, depression, alienation,
stress, exacerbated personal problems and situations, financial problems, dissatisfaction, disappointment, lack of fulfill-
ment, unrealized hopes, aging, loss, gain, fear, anxiety, terror,

guilt, and unresolved worry plague many of us. Present perhaps all year long, tensions increase with the expectation that somehow, in some way, the holiday will make it "all better." The season itself does little or nothing to solve the problems in our lives. Yet many of us annually perpetuate the fantasy that this year it will be different. The responsibility for creating emotional comfort rests with the individual, not the season. Changing our belief from "the holiday will make it better" to "I will make it better" is the first major step in managing holiday stress and preventing postholiday letdown.

Twenty Steps for Avoiding Holiday Crisis

1. Be realistic in your expectations about holidays and celebrations. Keep the euphemisms about the holiday in balance, and accept things as they are at the moment. Remember that acceptance does not necessarily mean agreement.
2. Remember, it is not what the holiday does for us, but what we do with the holiday that makes the difference. Use these events to build family unity, strengthen the bonds between family members, and remember loved ones who are far away.
3. Recognize that you are responsible for your life and that nothing and no one can be responsible for you. Saying to yourself, "If only Bob were here, everything would be OK," merely sidesteps your getting on with your life as necessary.
4. Live year-round, and especially at this season, by the present realities, not by your fantasy of how you want things to be.
5. Look to yourself as the source of your well-being and happiness.
6. Spend realistically. Give realistically. Going into debt will not create a "perfect" holiday or celebration.
7. Put gift giving and tasks in perspective. Remember that people are more important than things and events.
8. Recognize your grown children as adults.

9. If necessary, remind your parents that you are an adult.

10. Clarify family expectations long before the holiday season. Communicate feelings, exchange ideas, discuss arrangements, and check schedules; include all family members as appropriate. Avoid assumptions.

11. If you are planning a visit with your parents, make your expectations clear. Let your parents know you intend to visit with friends outside the family. Alert your parents to arrangements you might be considering. Avoid assumptions about baby-sitting, sleeping arrangements, transportation, and so on. "Home for the holidays" can be either a nightmare or a lovely experience. Consideration, fairness, clarity, careful planning, and shared feelings help determine a visit's success.

12. Invite your parents to your home for the holiday.

13. Acknowledge and allow for the feelings you experience. What you feel is very real. Allow yourself to miss loved ones who are away, and allow your children to express their feelings. Remember, it is all right to let your children see your feelings; it may help them learn more about handling theirs.

14. Share the work of holiday events. Assuming all the responsibility often results in victimhood.

15. Manage your time. Learn to say no when saying yes would be unrealistic.

16. Stick to regular diet and sleep routines as much as possible.

17. To avoid letdown, plan some interesting activities for after the holidays.

18. If you are in counseling, stay in counseling during the holiday season.

19. Learn to appreciate who and what you have rather than wishing you had someone or something else.

20. Enjoy this particular time of year, and this particular time of your life. It will never happen again.

CHAPTER NINE

GRIEF

1. Be aware that
   a. Grief is a normal emotional response to the loss of anything one values.
   b. Most crises involve loss.
   c. Every crisis involves an element of grief.
   d. The following elements determine the effects of grief on sufferers:
      (1) The intensity of the emotions experienced
      (2) The personal value connected to the loss
      (3) The sufferer's perception of the long-term effects created by the loss
2. Encourage and allow sufferers to express emotions without your judging them.

Mr. Jones: I retired a month ago after thirty-five years at the same company.

Intervener: I see such sadness in your eyes.

Mr. Jones: I can't stop crying. It's like my whole world just stopped . . . I feel so ashamed because everybody keeps telling me how lucky I am now that I can do anything I

want. I want to go back to being somebody . . . I want
to feel important and alive! I'm just waiting to die.

3. Let sufferers take the time necessary to express feelings before addressing options.

Intervener: Mr. Smith, you said that no one understands
what you're going through.

Mr. Smith: I've been offered a partnership in an aggressive,
well-established firm.

Intervener: What does that offer mean to you?

Mr. Smith: A lot more pain. You see, I'll have to move
to the West Coast.

Intervener: And what does that mean?

Mr. Smith: I just got over a bad divorce . . . I lost my wife,
the house, a lot of things important to me. My parents
live here now. This move means giving up more things
and more people . . . Financially, I can't afford not to
go . . . But I can't give up anything more.

Intervener: I hear how hard this decision is for you. There
are lots of feelings about moving and giving things up
that are important to you.

4. Assure sufferers that their emotions are normal and
acceptable.

Mrs. Brown: My husband died six weeks ago. I don't think
I want to go on anymore either.

Intervener: I'm sorry for your pain, Mrs. Brown. What do
you need right now?

Mrs. Brown: You're the only one who has asked me that.
Everybody else is so busy telling me what I should do
and what I should feel. I have had to be brave so I
wouldn't hurt anybody's feelings or worry my children.
I'm about to crack up!

Intervener: It's hard to keep up appearances.

Mrs. Brown: Please, just let me be me for a little while.
Just let me be me.

Intervener: Take your time. I'm here.

5. Assure sufferers that they can live through a lonely, painful experience.

Intervener: I hear the pain. I don't know exactly what you're experiencing, but I know you are hurting a great deal. I know you can get through this.

6. Let sufferers talk about feelings of guilt that might be associated with the crisis. Accept the validity of the guilt feelings just as you do the validity of other feelings expressed.
7. Allow sufferers to express anger and resentment about the loss. Assure them that these feelings are normal.
8. Remain caring, interested, and nonjudgmental.
9. Reach out to sufferers in appropriate ways.
10. Reach out physically only with permission.

WHAT SUFFERERS MIGHT EXPERIENCE DURING THE GRIEF PROCESS

Feeling off balance
Dizziness
Feeling uncoordinated
Erratic appetite
Disturbed sleep patterns
Feeling drugged without having taken drugs or medication
Feeling "out of sync" with one's own body
Irritability
Anger
Feeling disconnected from family, friends, and associates
Feeling disoriented
Rage from deep within one's own body
Feeling as though one is "falling apart" physically and emotionally
Feeling out of control
Deep sadness
Hopelessness

Feeling unwilling to make decisions and incapable of making them

Feeling that nothing has meaning and nothing matters

Feeling frozen in time and space

Feeling that all activity, no matter how limited, is too much effort

Confusion

Embarrassment about feelings

Guilt

An overwhelming sense of panic that nothing will ever feel right again

Feeling of spinning around but getting nowhere

Resentment that the loss has occurred

Relief that the ordeal leading to the final loss is over, and then guilt at feeling relieved

Feeling empty

Feeling numb

Feeling pushed down, buried, and very small

Turmoil associated with new or competing emotions

Ambivalence

Euphoria one moment and depression the next

SELF-INTERVENTION FOR SUFFERERS

Interveners should help sufferers to do the following:

1. Feel their own feelings. Let the feelings be whatever they are.
2. Avoid major changes that will require being uprooted physically or emotionally from loved ones, support systems, and that which is familiar and safe.
3. Put major decisions on hold.
4. Rely on the security of the familiar.
5. Set realistic expectations concerning work, home, chores, family obligations, and all other areas of life.
6. Seek out those people who are helpful and comforting and avoid, where possible, those who exacerbate

the sufferer's discomfort. Being well-intentioned does not necessarily translate into helpful behavior.

7. Recognize that the death of a significant other creates a sense of helplessness in survivors. Sufferers should identify those areas of life over which they have control and exercise that control immediately.

8. Maintain a daily routine. Persons suffering from grief should get up, get dressed, get out, and get moving every morning. This helps give the sufferer a sense of purpose and direction.

9. Care for themselves as follows:
   a. If work schedules do not permit rest during the day, arrange a routine after or before work to allow for extra rest as needed.
   b. Take appropriate vitamins to supplement the diet and minimize stress.
   c. Exercise daily to relieve tension.
   d. Walk daily and allow the senses of touch, smell, feeling, hearing, and sight to be energizers.

10. Let the process of recovery take as long as it takes.

11. Discover and use personal strengths.

COPING WITH
SEPARATION AND THE UNKNOWN

Interveners should help sufferers do the following:

1. Concentrate on the present.
2. Avoid trying to focus on the distant future.
3. Live for today.
4. Enjoy family and social relationships, and allow talk about thoughts and feelings as needed.
5. Finish projects previously started. If none are in progress, start a project and find enjoyment in it.
6. View each day as a victory.
7. Remember that each of us copes in different ways. People should find the best way by listening to their needs.

8. Accept personal responsibility for life as a way of helping oneself.
9. Participate actively in daily routines.
10. Set realistic goals.
11. Reach out to others and let them know the sufferer's wants, needs, and concerns.
12. Accept responsibility for their own frame of mind.
13. Set the tone for others with whom they associate.
14. Work with family, friends, and co-workers to help build and maintain a sense of control, purpose, and hope.
15. Encourage honest, open communication.
16. Remember that there will be good times and bad times.
17. Focus on the good and never lose hope that more good times lie ahead.
18. Share thoughts and feelings only when they wish to.
19. Be aware that sometimes talking with others eases emotional weight.
20. Remember that talking to others can provide new insight into dealing with a specific problem or situation.
21. Remember that if they cannot talk to family or friends, perhaps a professionally trained counselor would be helpful.
22. Recognize that self-help groups and sharing of common concerns can aid in the healing process.
23. Remember that letting feelings out with others can be a great release.
24. Try to live each day as fully as possible.
25. Discover that some concerns can be eased with current information, emotional support, knowledge, faith, and love.
26. Know that a decision to make the most of life, even in the face of separation, can help them.
27. Recognize that communication with loved ones will keep the sufferer in touch with significant others and with the world around them.

28. Live with a sense of purpose and the hope that good relationships will continue and that family, friends, and key support persons will be available to provide needed support.
29. Choose small goals and constructive ways to use time.
30. Ask "What is important to me right now?" and "What do I cherish?"
31. Think of the needs of other families, their own family, friends, and others who are important.
32. Keep a daily journal of feelings, thoughts, and experiences.
33. Direct personal energy into living each day as it comes and make each day count by what they put into it.
34. Try to live as normally as possible.
35. Keep close at hand things that have always provided enjoyment, such as photos, art, music, magazines, and books.
36. Surround themselves with familiar things.
37. Keep up with local and national news.
38. Ask others to go out for a meal or movie or to just drop by for a visit.
39. Recognize that on some days the sufferer may want to be left alone and that this is OK.
40. Maintain self-respect even though it may sometimes seem difficult.

THE CRISIS REVISITED: COPING WITH THE AFTERMATH

For many, a crisis stirs painful memories of previous crises. Crisis victims are required to deal with feelings that either were never resolved or were thought to be resolved. The emotional wounds seem fresh, and the bleeding recurs.

The following are some reactions common to people who experience traumatic stress as a result of a tragic incident. You may have these reactions if you have survived or witnessed a traumatic event. These reactions may vary in intensity and duration and may occur whether or not you are physically injured. Although these thoughts, feelings, and behaviors can be very upsetting, it is important to remember that they are normal reactions to an abnormal situation.

Thoughts

- Repeated thoughts or memories of the event
- Recurring dreams or nightmares
- Being caught off guard by a person, place, or event that reminds you of the original event
- Reconstructing the event in your mind in an effort to regain a sense of control
- Trouble concentrating or remembering things
- Questioning your view of the world or your spiritual beliefs

Feelings

- Feeling pervasive fear
- Feeling emotionally numb or withdrawn
- Lacking enjoyment in everyday activities
- Feeling depressed
- Distrusting others
- Feeling anger, including a desire for revenge or vengeance

Behaviors

- Being extremely alert or startling easily
- Being overprotective of your own and your family's safety

CHAPTER TEN

LEGAL IMPLICATIONS OF CRISIS INTERVENTION[1]

Although Crisis Intervention and the intervener's function is not about the legalities involved, one should at least consider how these legalities relate to intervention. We live in a litigious society, where self-responsibility is often lacking and lawsuits are often the remedy. Lawsuits can be filed against anyone, at almost any time and for almost any reason if a plaintiff feels that a personal wrong or injury has been caused. Generally such claims are brought under civil or tort law rather than under criminal law. That is, civil offenses or torts have been committed against individuals rather than against the state.

Nothing said here can completely prevent such action or insulate the intervener from all exposure. However, some guidelines, procedures, and areas of awareness can ease the potential legal burden of the intervener and allow everyone to get on with the real job—effective assistance to those in crisis.

[1]Nothing stated in this chapter should be construed in any way to be legally definitive or to replace your own research into the laws of your state and city. Nor should you take this information as legal advice or as negation of the importance of seeking competent counsel from a licensed attorney.

Not all areas of concern to interveners will be dealt with extensively in this chapter. However, all interveners should be familiar with the following issues and how the laws regarding these issues apply to them.

Interveners may need to do individual research to ascertain the information they need. For that purpose legal references are provided at the end of this chapter. The following are some issues that may apply to interveners:

Negligence
Informed consent
Confidentiality
Exceptions to confidentiality
Duty to warn
Recordkeeping
Right to privacy
Right to refuse intervention
"Good Samaritan" laws
Standards of care
Abandonment
Consent to intervention
Actual consent
Implied consent

To work effectively in the Crisis Intervention field, interveners must recognize that they are bound by the laws of society and that, even under extreme circumstances, such proscriptions cannot be ignored without consequence. "Good Samaritan" laws generally protect those whose intent it is to assist others in times of crisis. Such assistance must always be reasonable and prudent and must be based on the level and kind of training the intervener has received and now applies. To such standards of care we must adhere.

For example, the Good Samaritan Law of the State of Texas (Chapter 74 of the Civil Practice and Remedies Code, 1991) states that

(a) A person who in good faith administers emergency care at the scene of an emergency or in a hospital is not liable in civil damages for an act performed during the emergency unless the act is willfully or wantonly negligent.

(b) This section does not apply to care administered:
  (1) for or in expectation of remuneration;
  (2) by a person who was at the scene of the emergency because he or a person he represents as an agent was soliciting business or seeking to perform a service for remuneration;
  (3) by a person who regularly administers care in a hospital emergency room; or
  (4) by an admitting physician or a treating physician associated by the admitting physician of the patient bringing a health-care liability claim.

Similar Good Samaritan laws exist in many other states. Interveners should be familiar with the content of the law that applies to them.

Unless an intervener has a preexisting duty to intervene in another person's crisis, the law does not require that anyone intervene in the crisis of anyone else. Police, fire fighters, and emergency service personnel usually have a preexisting duty because they are hired to perform such tasks. Further, once an intervener has begun an intervention with another person, the intervention must continue unless the intervener is relieved by someone with greater competency. Not to do so could be construed as abandonment and could expose the intervener to legal consequences.

Liability is generally determined by the courts; therefore, the concept of negligence, or malpractice, must be understood by all interveners. In Crisis Intervention, good intentions are often not enough to avoid legal problems.

Negligence may result when an intervener assumes a duty of reasonable care for a victim and then breaches that duty, thereby causing damage or further injury to the victim. Generally, except when interveners have a preexisting duty, they are not required to intervene with a victim. Their moral or ethical values may dictate otherwise, however.

If an intervener, with or without a preexisting duty, decides to intervene with a sufferer, the intervener may assume a duty of reasonable care for that sufferer. Further, such a duty may be seen as assumed if the intervener acts in a way that creates a foreseeable risk to the victim.

For example, an intervener decides to take action to assist a sufferer. The action resulting from that decision creates a foreseeable risk to the victim; that is, the intervener's action could adversely affect the victim. In this case, the intervener has assumed a duty of reasonable care. If the usual procedure in this particular intervention is to remove the victim from the crisis situation, and the intervener decides against such movement, such a decision might cause additional injury to the victim.

If, as a result of such action, the victim is injured further or is damaged in other ways, the intervener may be said to have breached the duty of reasonable care and to have acted negligently. In such a case, a court might be asked to decide the intervener's liability based on the damages caused. Generally, the measure of negligence the court applies will be the standard of care given by the intervener. It must also be shown that the intervener's actions are the proximate or direct cause of the injury that the sufferer sustains.

Conversely, should the intervener decide not to intervene, lack of action would not create a duty of reasonable care because the intervener's actions—or inaction—would not have created risk to the victim other than that already experienced by the victim at that time. Even though inaction might allow the victim's suffering to continue, no duty of reasonable care has been created because in this case there is no duty to rescue. However, for police, fire fighters, and emergency medical service personnel, the exact opposite may be true because of their preexisting duty to act in such cases.

The following guidelines are intended to help interveners avoid the difficulties of legal confrontations and to keep them where they belong, doing what they are best trained to do—serving in the field, helping victims manage the crises in their lives.

LEGAL GUIDELINES IN CRISIS INTERVENTION

1. Always treat people as human beings, not just as cases.
2. Show respect to all with whom you are involved.
3. Intervene within the limits of your background and training. Do not exceed those limits, thereby committing the illegal practice of medicine, law, or psychology.
4. Unless you have a preexisting duty to intervene, consider carefully whether you want to perform an intervention.
5. Once you have begun to intervene, don't stop.
6. Discontinue your intervention only if you are relieved by someone with greater skill than your own.
7. Determine how the Good Samaritan laws relate to the types of intervention in which you may be involved.
8. If in doubt about your legal standing, contact a competent attorney and discuss your concerns.
9. Maintain confidentiality of all information you obtain about a crisis victim. Understand under what special circumstances you may have a duty to warn another person or to otherwise breach intervener-victim confidentiality.
10. Document everything you say and do with a victim. This may assist you later if you or your procedures are challenged.
11. Maintain your competency. Update your training and credentials as required.
12. Whenever possible, obtain the victim's consent before you assist with the crisis. If in doubt, ask!
13. If emergency circumstances do not allow for actual consent by the victim, you may be able to proceed under the concept of implied consent. However, in such circumstances, do only what is absolutely necessary to effectively intervene or rescue.

14. Do not disturb a crime scene. If you cannot avoid doing so, note exact locations of whatever is moved so that later you can give such information to proper authorities.

15. If you must search a victim's personal effects, try to have one or two witnesses present to observe your actions.

16. Know what you are required to report to the authorities. Requirements vary from state to state. (For example, child abuse must be reported in most states.)

17. Know the legal procedures in your jurisdiction for admissions for psychiatric care. Usually admissions are categorized as either voluntary or involuntary.

18. Remember that crisis interveners are not usually immune from observation of motor vehicle laws or from legal responsibility for vehicular accidents or property damage.

19. Respect the victim's right to privacy.

20. If the victim is a minor, obtain the permission of one of the parents before intervening. If this is not possible, you may be able to proceed under the doctrine of implied consent, as you would with an adult.

21. Be honest and open with victims.

22. Always think through what you will do, toward what end you will be doing it, what risks are present, and what safeguards you will apply.

23. Prepare yourself with knowledge of the law as well as of Crisis Intervention skills.

24. Remember that liability can be effected by both acts of commission and acts of omission.

25. Respect a sufferer's right to refuse your intervention.

26. Before entering a crisis victim's domain, dwelling, or office, request that person's permission. Know when the laws of your locality permit you to enter without permission.

27. If you are the director or supervisor of a Crisis Intervention agency, be sure all interveners and hotline workers understand and can apply agency policies and procedures.

28. Within Crisis Intervention agencies, develop specific, understandable policies and procedures that clearly regulate and illustrate how intervention is to be performed.

29. As an agency director or supervisor, adhere to agency policy and insist that interveners do likewise.

30. Incorporate agency policies and legal issues into the training of crisis interveners.

LEGAL REFERENCES

Arizona Revised Statute for Privileged Communications, § 32-2085 (1965). (Privileged Communications)

Buwa v. *Smith*, 84-1905 NMB (1986). (Duty to Warn)

Canterbury v. *Spense*, 464 F. 2d. 772 (D.C. Cir. 1972), cert. den. 93 S.Ct. 560 (1972). (Informed Consent)

Cutter v. *Brownbridge*, Cal. Ct. App., 1st Dist. 330 (1986). (Privileged Communications)

Hales v. *Pittman*, 118 Ariz. 305, 576 P. 2d. 493 (1978). (Informed Consent)

McDonald v. *Clinger*, 446 N.Y.S. 2d. 801 (1982). (Confidentiality)

McIntosh v. *Milano*, 403 A. 2d. 500 (N.J.S.Ct. 1979). (Duty to Warn)

New Jersey Revised Statutes, New Jersey Marriage Counseling Act, Annotated § 45: 8B-29 (1969). (Exceptions to Confidentiality)

People v. *District Court, City and County of Denver*, 719 P.2d. 722 (Colo. 1986). (Privileged Communications)

Rodriguez v. *Jackson*, 118 Ariz. 13, 574 P. 2d. 481 (App. 1978). (Informed Consent)

Sard v. *Hardy*, 291 Md. 432, 379 A. 2d. 1014 (1977). (Informed Consent)

Tarasoff v. *Regents of California*, 131 Cal. Rptr. 14, 551 P. 2d. 334 (1976). (Duty to Warn)

Whitree v. *State of New York*, 56 Misc. 2d. 693, 290 N.Y.S. 2s. 486 (1968). (Record Keeping)

APPENDIX

COMMUNICATING EFFECTIVELY WITH THOSE IN CRISIS

Before a problem can be managed, the intervener must determine what the problem is. Often, more than one problem may be present in a situation. When this occurs, the following six questions may be asked to determine the priority for intervention.

1. Which problem is of most immediate concern?
2. Which problem would prove most damaging if not treated immediately?
3. Which problem can be most quickly resolved?
4. Which problem must be dealt with first before others may be handled?
5. What resources for handling problems are available?
6. What barriers and obstacles will hinder problem solving?[1]

Although it is necessary to answer all the preceding questions, if the intervener is to help manage the victim's crisis,

[1]From *Emotional First Aid* by E. S. Rosenbluh. Copyright © 1981 by Rosenbluh. This and all other quotes from the same source are reprinted with permission. Dr. E. S. Rosenbluh.

the intervener must be able to acquire the needed information quickly and accurately. This means that the intervener must listen actively to the victim's total message and give the victim full concentration and undivided attention. Further, the intervener must sift through the person's words to gain information and insight into the victim's problems and views of those problems.

Every communication contains three messages: a content message, a feeling message, and a meaning message. The content message provides information about what the sender believes, thinks, or perceives the situation to be. The feeling message conveys the nature and intensity of the sender's emotion about the situation. The meaning message concerns the behavior or situation that has generated the feeling. Usually the person who sends the communication implies, rather than explicitly states, the behavior or situation that creates the feeling. The intervener must try to infer what the behavior or situation is.

Rosenbluh (1981) explained that when another person communicates with you, distortion can occur in three areas:

1. What the other person means to say
2. What the other person actually says
3. What you, as the intervener, believe you hear

The present discussion is concerned with what interveners think they hear. The key to effective listening is accurately hearing the feeling and meaning behind the content of communication. The skill discussed here is *empathy*. Empathy is one's ability to enter the other person's world and to reflect this understanding to the person. Empathy, as Rosenbluh (1981) pointed out, contains two elements:

- *Passive:* the ability to hear the facts contained in the words and the feelings contained in the other person's body language, intensity, and tone
- *Active:* the ability to reflect this understanding to the other person in a manner that generates warmth, trust, and a willingness to be open

CLARIFICATION

Sometimes a victim will make a statement that the intervener does not fully understand. At other times, the victim's words and nonverbal behavior may not agree. At that point the intervener focuses on the misunderstanding and tries to clarify the statement in question before continuing with the interview. Interveners must never assume that they understand what the victim means. Two people can witness the same event and describe it very differently. Conversely, two people can have very different experiences and relate these experiences similarly. Interveners must be sure they know precisely what the victim is talking about. To do so, the intervener must press the sufferer to clarify any vague or ambiguous statements. An intervener cannot work effectively with a victim unless both the intervener and the victim are talking about the same crisis.

Clarification Techniques

Interveners can use the following four techniques to help victims clarify their statements:

1. *Repeating key words.* Using this technique, the intervener repeats key words or phrases that the victim uses and that the intervener does not clearly understand. By emphasizing a certain word or phrase, the intervener focuses attention on a particular thought or feeling and encourages the victim to explain it in more detail.

For example:

Victim: I feel helpless when I think of all these bills . . . and I have no income.
Intervener: Helpless?
Victim: I just don't care anymore. I feel so isolated and depressed.

Intervener: You don't care anymore?
or   You feel isolated?
or   You feel depressed?

Interveners should use this technique carefully. When used too frequently, repeating what the person just said can sound like a gimmick. The intervener's parroting may make the victim distrustful and uneasy. Repetition is, however, a useful tool when used cautiously.

2. *Restatement.* The intervener can rephrase the victim's statements in such a way that the person is encouraged to clarify what was said.

For example:

Victim: I'm behind in all my bills, and my father, who is a local banker, told me it was embarrassing him because my creditors have been calling him, too.
Intervener: So you're having financial problems, and you are feeling heavy family pressure to find a solution.

When an intervener uses restatement, the victim will often respond by talking about the most pressing area of concern. Using restatement also encourages the victim to explain the situation in more detail. This additional information will help the intervener understand what the victim is thinking and feeling.

3. *Direct method.* Perhaps the most direct method of eliciting information is for interveners to admit that they are confused or puzzled about the victim's statement and to ask the victim for clarification so that better understanding will result. This technique has the added advantage of letting the victim know that the intervener is interested in what is being said. Additionally, this kind of communication helps to build trust in the intervener-victim relationship.

4. *Asking questions.* An intervener can obtain a clearer idea of the other person's meaning simply by asking

questions. When interveners want more information, they can ask "open" questions. To pinpoint specific items, interveners can ask "closed" questions. A *closed question* can be answered with a simple "yes" or "no." An *open question* allows for amplification of meaning by the respondent.

For example:

Victim: I don't know what my husband is talking about.
Intervener: What does he say that you don't understand? [open question]
Victim: All I want is the best for my child. I am so miserable and feel so defeated that I want to kill myself.
Intervener: How would killing yourself help your child? [open question]
or
Do you have a suicide plan in mind? [closed question]

The closed-question technique is particularly useful when an intervener is fairly sure of what additional information is needed.

Identifying the victim's concerns during the assessment and attempting to clarify the real issues involved help both the victim and the intervener to better understand the total situation that must be dealt with.

USING QUESTIONS EFFECTIVELY

Asking questions to obtain accurate information in an intervention is both necessary and helpful. The intervener must be careful, however, to pace the questions carefully so as not to increase the victim's stress level. Bombarding victims with a series of questions could confuse and frustrate them. Also, allow sufficient time for the victim to answer. Ask the questions in a nonthreatening, nonaccusatory tone.

DEALING WITH SILENCE

The intervener should know how to use silence during an intervention. For some interveners, silence is deadly. It may seem as if nothing is happening, and this can cause the intervener great discomfort. Interveners should handle silence by being silent themselves while observing the victim's behavior and what the victim is *not* saying.

RESPONDING EFFECTIVELY

Responding to another person's feelings is a delicate process. In gathering information from victims, the intervener must handle the victims' feelings with care and concern. If the intervener wants a victim to continue talking about facts pertinent to the problem, the intervener cannot judge, use logic, or give advice. The individual's feelings must be legitimized. The following example illustrates ineffective response to emotions:

Boy: I can't stand my father. He's been mean to me all my life.

Intervener: That's unfair. What would you do if anything happened to him? You'd feel awful to have said things like that.

In this instance, communication has been effectively shut off. The intervener has passed judgment and shamed the boy instead of seeking the root of the hostility.

GUIDELINES FOR EFFECTIVE COMMUNICATIONS IN CRISES

1. **Listen effectively.**
- Fully hear what the other person is saying.
- Maintain eye contact if at all possible.
- Let the other person talk freely.
- Try to comprehend what the other person is saying.

- Listen for both feelings and content.
- Paraphrase the other's statements to gain clarification.
- Ask for clarification when necessary.
- Don't let your own feelings get in the way of understanding what the other person is trying to say.

2. **Respond descriptively.**

- Don't be evaluative in your response; evaluative statements tend to elicit defensiveness.
- Keep in mind that "rightness" or "wrongness" may not be the issue.
- Remember, effective communication is not a contest; a "win or lose" mentality is inappropriate.
- Learn all you can about the other person's thoughts and feelings.
- Let the other person know some things about you.
- Use descriptive statements and reveal your reactions to the other person.

3. **Use your own feelings.**

- Remember that feelings are important in communicating and that they are always present.
- Practice expressing your feelings.
- Take responsibility for your feelings.
- Use "I" messages rather than "you" messages; "I" messages reduce threat to the other person.
- Use descriptive statements that contain feelings.
- Be clear and specific about your feelings.

4. **Assess needs.**

- Consider the needs of all involved.
- Address issues over which the victim has actual control.
- Avoid being judgmental and critical; avoid preaching.

5. **Make timely responses.**

- Deliver responses at the time they are most important.
- Deliver responses as soon as possible after the behavior that requires response.
- Do not store up old concerns for later discussion.

- Do not use old or saved concerns as a weapon.
- Assess whether the other person is ready to handle your responses at this time.
- Consider delaying responses on sensitive issues until you are in a more appropriate setting.
- Discuss emotional issues in private.
- Practice communication skills for greatest effectiveness.

LISTENING

During conversations with victims, keep in mind the following items about the importance of listening:

1. Listening is basic to successful communications.
2. Listening requires responsiveness.
3. Listening enables the listener to know more about the speaker.
4. Listening encourages expression.
5. Listening allows exploration of both feelings and content.
6. Listening helps establish trust between the parties.
7. Listening allows greater accuracy of communication.
8. Listening requires practice and is not always easy to learn.
9. Listening includes listening for content, feelings, and point of view.
10. Listening lets the speaker relax.
11. Attitudes and feelings may be conveyed nonverbally.

When you listen, remember to do the following:

1. Attend to verbal content.
2. Attend to nonverbal cues.
3. Hear and observe.
4. Attend to the feelings expressed by the speaker.
5. Don't think about other things when you are listening to someone.
6. Don't listen with only "half an ear."

7. Become attuned to the speaker's verbal and non-verbal messages.
8. Note any extra emphasis the speaker places on certain words.
9. Notice the speaker's speech patterns and recurring themes.

NONVERBAL COMMUNICATIONS

The following are examples of nonverbal acts a speaker may use to communicate:

- Sighing
- Flipping through papers
- Wincing
- Looking around, up, or down
- Smoking
- Chewing gum
- Yawning
- Tapping a finger or foot
- Frowning
- Displaying nervousness
- Avoiding eye contact
- Saying nothing
- Making jerky gestures
- Dressing sloppily
- Blinking rapidly
- Constantly looking at a clock or watch
- Showing favoritism
- Acting bored
- Being drunk

Certain nonverbal cues can indicate a specific attitude. Some examples follow.

Nonverbal Cues that May Indicate Openness

- Uncrossed legs
- Open hands

- Unbuttoned coat, or unbuttoning the coat
- Hands spread apart
- Palms up
- Leaning forward

Nonverbal Cues that May Indicate Defensiveness

- Fists closed
- Arms crossed in front of individual
- Legs crossed
- One leg over the chair arm

Nonverbal Cues that May Indicate Cooperation

- Opening coat
- Tilted head
- Sitting on the edge of a chair
- Eye contact
- Hand-to-face gestures
- Leaning forward

Nonverbal Cues that May Indicate Evaluating

- Head tilted
- Chin stroking
- Looking over glasses
- Pacing
- Pinching the bridge of the nose

Nonverbal Cues that May Indicate Readiness

- Hands on hips
- Leaning forward
- Confident speech
- Moving closer to the other person

Nonverbal Cues that May Indicate Suspicion

- Lack of eye contact
- Glancing sideways at the other person
- Body apparently pointed toward exit from area
- Touching the bridge of the nose
- Rubbing the ears
- Rubbing the eyes

Nonverbal Cues that May Indicate Confidence

- Elevating oneself by sitting on a higher chair or standing on a platform
- Finger "steepling"
- Hands clasped behind the back
- Feet on a desk or table
- Leaning on an object
- Clucking sound
- Leaning back, with both hands supporting the neck

Both the following list and Figure A.1 are guides that an intervener can show to victims who are having trouble identifying their feelings.

Feelings that Persons Have But Often Fail to Identify

Abandoned	Bad	Charmed
Adequate	Betrayed	Cheated
Affectionate	Bitter	Cheerful
Ambivalent	Blissful	Childish
Angry	Bold	Clever
Annoyed	Bored	Combative
Anxious	Brave	Competitive
Apathetic	Calm	Condemned
Astounded	Capable	Confused
Awed	Challenged	Conspicuous

Contented	Glad	Mad
Cruel	Good	Mean
Crushed	Gratified	Miserable
Deceitful	Greedy	Mystical
Defeated	Grief	Naughty
Delighted	Guilty	Nervous
Desirous	Happy	Nice
Despair	Hate	Nutty
Destructive	Heavenly	Obnoxious
Determined	Helpful	Obsessed
Different	Helpless	Odd
Disappointed	High	Outraged
Discontented	Homesick	Overwhelmed
Distraught	Horrible	Pain
Disturbed	Hurt	Panicked
Divided	Hysterical	Peaceful
Dominated	Ignored	Persecuted
Eager	Imposed upon	Petrified
Ecstatic	Impressed	Pity
Embarrassed	Infatuated	Pleasant
Empty	Infuriated	Pleased
Enchanted	Inspired	Pressured
Energetic	Intimidated	Proud
Enjoyment	Irritated	Quarrelsome
Envious	Isolated	Rage
Evil	Jealousy	Refreshed
Exasperated	Joyous	Rejected
Excited	Jumpy	Relaxed
Exhausted	Kind	Relieved
Fascinated	Lazy	Remorse
Fearful	Lecherous	Restless
Flustered	Left out	Righteous
Foolish	Lonely	Sad
Frantic	Longing	Sated
Free	Love	Satisfied
Frightened	Loving	Scared
Frustrated	Low	Screwed up
Furious	Lustful	Sexy

Shocked
Silly
Skeptical
Sneaky
Solemn
Sorrowful
Spiteful
Startled
Stingy
Stuffed
Stupid
Stunned

Suffering
Sure
Sympathetic
Talkative
Tempted
Tense
Terrible
Terrified
Threatened
Tired
Trapped
Troubled

Ugly
Uneasy
Unsettled
Violent
Vehement
Vulnerable
Vivacious
Weepy
Wicked
Wonderful
Worried

Figure A.1
How do you feel today?

BIBLIOGRAPHY

ARIZONA REVISED STATUTE FOR PRIVILEGED COMMUNICATIONS, § 32-2085 (1965).

BUWA v. SMITH, 84-1905 NMB (1986).

CANTERBURY v. SPENSE, 464 F. 2d. 772 (D.C. Cir. 1972), cert. den. 93 S.Ct. 560 (1972).

CORSINI, R. J. (1981). *Innovative Psychotherapies.* New York: Wiley Interscience.

CUTTER v. BROWNBRIDGE, Cal. Ct. App., 1st Dist. (1986).

EVARTS, W. R., GREENSTONE, J. L., KIRKPATRICK, G., & LEVITON, S. C. (1984). *Winning through accommodation: The mediator's handbook.* Dubuque, IA: Kendall/Hunt.

FOWLER, W. R., & GREENSTONE, J. L. (1983). Hostage negotiations. In R. Corsini (Ed.), *Encyclopedia of psychology.* New York: Wiley.

FOWLER, W. R., & GREENSTONE, J. L. (1987). Hostage negotiations for police. In R. Corsini (Ed.), *Concise encyclopedia of psychology.* New York: Wiley Interscience.

FOWLER, W. R. & GREENSTONE, J. L. (1989). *Crisis intervention compendium.* Littleton, MA: Copley.

GREENSTONE, J. L. (1969). Tuning in with our children. *The Single Parent, 1,* 1–5.

GREENSTONE, J. L. (1970). *The meaning of psychology: A human subject.* Dubuque, IA: Kendall/Hunt.

GREENSTONE, J. L. (1971). The crisis of discipline. *The Single Parent, 2,* 5–10.

GREENSTONE, J. L. (1973). Parent's voice . . . child's choice. *The Single Parent, 2,* 5–8.

GREENSTONE, J. L. (1978). An interdisciplinary approach to marital disputes arbitration: The Dallas plan. *Conciliation Courts Review, 16,* 7–15.

GREENSTONE, J. L. (1981). Job related stress: Is it killing you? *National Law Journal, 4,* 30–34.

GREENSTONE, J. L. (1981, July). *Hostage survival.* Paper presented at the meeting of the Plano Amateur Radio Club, Dallas, TX.

GREENSTONE, J. L. (1981, October). *Crisis intervention: Stress and the police officer.* Paper presented at the meeting of the Society for Police and Criminal Psychology, Baton Rouge, LA.

GREENSTONE, J. L. (1982, November). *Crisis intervention and what to do if taken hostage.* Paper presented at the meeting of the Protestant Men's Club, Dallas, TX.

GREENSTONE, J. L. (1983, February 13). The divorce referee. *Dallas Morning News,* "Today" section, p. 20.

GREENSTONE, J. L. (1984). The crisis at Christmas. *Emotional First Aid: A Journal of Crisis Intervention, 1,* 21–29.

GREENSTONE, J. L. (1984, December 13). Holiday doesn't replace therapy: Crisis steps to avoid. *Northwest Passage,* pp. 1–2.

GREENSTONE, J. L. (1986, June). *Alternatives in dispute resolution: Family and marital mediation.* Paper presented at the meeting of the Fifth International Congress of Family Therapy, Jerusalem, Israel.

GREENSTONE, J. L. (1986). The laws of terrorism. *Emotional First Aid: A Journal of Crisis Intervention, 3,* 150–160.

GREENSTONE, J. L. (1992). The art of negotiating: Tactics and negotiating techniques—the way of the past and the way of the future. *Command: Journal of the Texas Tactical Police Officers Association, 1,* 11–18.

GREENSTONE, J. L. (1992). The key to success for hostage negotiations teams: Training, training, and more training. *The Police Forum, 1,* 3–4.

GREENSTONE, J. L. (1992, April). *Mediation advocacy: A new concept in the arena of family dispute resolution.* Paper presented at the meeting of the Sixth International Congress on Family Therapy: Divorce and Remarriage Interdisciplinary Issues and Approaches, Jerusalem, Israel.

GREENSTONE, J. L., & LEVITON, S. C. (1979). *The crisis intervener's handbook, volume 1.* Dallas, TX: Crisis Management Workshops.

GREENSTONE, J. L., & LEVITON, S. C. (1979). *Crisis management and intervener survival.* Tulsa, OK: Affective House.

GREENSTONE, J. L., & LEVITON, S. C. (1979, July). *Intervention and emergency therapy in marriage and family crises.* Paper presented at the Third International Congress of Family Therapy and Family Life Education, Tel Aviv, Israel.

GREENSTONE, J. L., & LEVITON, S. C. (1979). *Stress reduction: Personal energy management.* Tulsa, OK: Affective House.

GREENSTONE, J. L., & LEVITON, S. C. (1980). *The crisis intervener's handbook, volume 2.* Dallas, TX: Rothschild.

GREENSTONE, J. L., & LEVITON, S. C. (1980). Crisis management: A basic concern. *The Crisis Intervener's Newsletter, 1,* 1–2.

GREENSTONE, J. L., & LEVITON, S. C. (1981). Crisis management and intervener survival. In R. Corsini (Ed.), *Innovative psychotherapies.* New York: Wiley Interscience.

GREENSTONE, J. L., & LEVITON, S. C. (1981). *Hotline: Crisis intervention directory.* New York: Facts on File.

GREENSTONE, J. L., & LEVITON, S. C. (1981). *Training the trainer.* Tulsa, OK: Affective House.

GREENSTONE, J. L., & LEVITON, S. C. (1982). *Crisis intervention: Handbook for interveners.* Dubuque, IA: Kendall/Hunt.

GREENSTONE, J. L., & LEVITON, S. C. (1983). Crisis intervention. In R. Corsini (Ed.), *Encyclopedia of psychology.* New York: Wiley.

GREENSTONE, J. L., & LEVITON, S. C. (1983, January). Divorce mediation. *D Magazine,* pp. 3–5.

GREENSTONE, J. L., & LEVITON, S. C. (1983, March). *Divorce mediation and the attorney.* Paper presented at the meeting of the Family Law Section of the Dallas Bar Association, Dallas, TX.

GREENSTONE, J. L., & LEVITON, S. C. (1983). Executive survival. In R. Corsini (Ed.), *Encyclopedia of psychology.* New York: Wiley.

GREENSTONE, J. L., & LEVITON, S. C. (1983, March). *Mediation: An alternative to litigation.* Paper presented at the meeting of the Academy of Criminal Justice Sciences, San Antonio, TX.

GREENSTONE, J. L., & LEVITON, S. C. (1983, July). *Mediation: Family dispute resolution.* Paper presented at the meeting of the Fourth International Congress of Family Therapy, Tel Aviv, Israel.

GREENSTONE, J. L., & LEVITON, S. C. (1984, March). *Divorce mediation: The way of the 80's.* Paper presented at the meeting of the Oklahoma Association of Marriage and Family Therapists, Tulsa, OK.

GREENSTONE, J. L., & LEVITON, S. C. (1984, September). *Crisis intervention in mediation.* Paper presented at the meeting of the National Conference on Peace and Conflict Resolution, St. Louis, MO.

GREENSTONE, J. L., & LEVITON, S. C. (1984, September). *Management mediation: The police officer's alternative to litigation.* Paper presented at the meeting of the First National Symposium on Police Psychological Services, Quantico, VA.

GREENSTONE, J. L., & LEVITON, S. C. (1984, December). *Crisis management for the mediator.* Paper presented at the meeting of the Second Annual Conference on Problem Solving through Mediation, Albany, NY.

GREENSTONE, J. L., & LEVITON, S. C. (1986, July). *The dispute mediator as crisis manager: Crisis intervention skills for the mediator in high stress, high risk situations.* Paper presented at the meeting of the Academy of Family Mediators, Minneapolis, MN.

GREENSTONE, J. L., & LEVITON, S. C. (1986). Intervention procedures. *Emotional First Aid: A Journal of Crisis Intervention, 3,* 100–110.

GREENSTONE, J. L., & LEVITON, S. C. (1986). Mediation: The police officer's alternative to litigation. In *Psychological services for law enforcement.* Washington, D.C.: U.S. Department of Justice, Federal Bureau of Investigation, U.S. Government Printing Office.

GREENSTONE, J. L., & LEVITON, S. C. (1986). Referrals: A key to successful crisis intervention. *Emotional First Aid: A Journal of Crisis Intervention, 3,* 75–80.

GREENSTONE, J. L., & LEVITON, S. C. (1987). Crisis intervention. In R. Corsini (Ed.), *Concise encyclopedia of psychology.* New York: Wiley Interscience.

GREENSTONE, J. L., & LEVITON, S. C. (1987, July). *Crisis intervention for mediators in high risk, high stress, potentially violent situations.* Paper presented at the meeting of the Academy of Family Mediators, New York, NY.

GREENSTONE, J. L., & LEVITON, S. C. (1987). Crisis management for mediators in high stress, high risk, potentially violent situations. *Mediation Quarterly, 3,* 20–30.

GREENSTONE, J. L., & LEVITON, S. C. (1987). Executive survival. In R. Corsini (Ed.), *Concise Encyclopedia of Psychology.* New York: Wiley Interscience.

GREENSTONE, J. L., & LEVITON, S. C. (1991). *Parents, kids, and war: Information designed to assist parents and children in handling war and its consequences.*

GREENSTONE, J. L., & LEVITON, S. C. (1992, April). *Crisis management for mediators in high stress, high risk, potentially violent family and divorce mediations.* Paper presented at the meeting of the Sixth International Congress on Family Therapy: Divorce and Remarriage Interdisciplinary Issues and Approaches, Jerusalem, Israel.

GREENSTONE, J. L., & ROSENBLUH, E. S. (1980). Evolution of the American Academy of Crisis Interveners and the Southwestern Academy of Crisis Interveners. *The Crisis Intervener's Newsletter, 1*, 13–14.

HALES v. PITTMAN, 118 Ariz. 305, 576 P. 2d. 493 (1978).

HENDRICKS, J., & GREENSTONE, J. L. (1982, March). *Crisis intervention in criminal justice.* Paper presented at the meeting of the Academy of Criminal Justice Sciences, Louisville, KY.

LEVITON, S. C., & GREENSTONE, J. L. (1980). Intervener survival: Dealing with the givens. *Emotional First Aid: A Journal of Crisis Intervention, 2*, 15–20.

LEVITON, S. C., & GREENSTONE, J. L. (1983). Conflict mediation. In R. Corsini (Ed.), *Encyclopedia of psychology.* New York: Wiley.

LEVITON, S. C., & GREENSTONE, J. L. (1983). Intervener survival. In R. Corsini (Ed.), *Encyclopedia of psychology.* New York: Wiley.

LEVITON, S. C., & GREENSTONE, J. L. (1984). Mediation in potential crisis situations. *Emotional First Aid: A Journal of Crisis Intervention, 1*, 150–155.

LEVITON, S. C., & GREENSTONE, J. L. (1984). Team intervention. *Emotional First Aid: A Journal of Crisis Intervention, 1*, 20–25.

LEVITON, S. C., & GREENSTONE, J. L. (1987). Conflict mediation. In R. Corsini (Ed.), *Concise encyclopedia of psychology.* New York: Wiley Interscience.

LEVITON, S. C., & GREENSTONE, J. L. (1987). Intervener survival. In R. Corsini (Ed.), *Concise encyclopedia of psychology.* New York: Wiley Interscience.

McDONALD v. CLINGER, 446 N.Y.S. 2d. 801 (1982).

McINTOSH v. MILANO, 403 A. 2d. 500 (N.J.S.Ct. 1979).

MITCHELL, J. T., & RESNIK, H. L. P. (1981). *Emergency response to crisis.* Bowie, MD: Brady.

MORDOCK, J. B., ELLIS, M. H., & GREENSTONE, J. L. (1969). The effects of group and individual therapy on sociometric choice of disturbed adolescents. *International Journal of Group Psychotherapy, 4*, 200–210.

PEDERSON, P. A. (1988). *A handbook for developing multicultural awareness.* New York: American Association for Counseling and Development.

PEOPLE v. DISTRICT COURT, CITY AND COUNTY OF DENVER, 719 P. 2d. 722 (Colo. 1986).

RODRIGUEZ v. JACKSON, 118 Ariz. 13, 574 P. 2d. 481 (App. 1978).

ROSENBLUH, E. S. (1981). *Emotional first aid.* Louisville, KY: American Academy of Crisis Interveners.

ROSENBLUH, E. S. (1986). *Crisis counseling: Emotional first aid.* Dubuque, IA: Kendall/Hunt.

SARD v. HARDY, 291 Md. 432, 379 A. 2d. 1014 (1977).

SLAIKEU, K. A. (1984). *Crisis intervention: A handbook for practice and research.* Boston: Allyn & Bacon.

TARASOFF v. REGENTS OF CALIFORNIA, 131 Cal. Rptr. 14, 551 P. 2d. 334 (1976).

WHITREE v. STATE OF NEW YORK, 56 Misc. 2d. 693, 290 N.Y.S. 2s. 486 (1968).